INTERNET AD
TH

30 DAY PLAN TO TAKE BACK YOUR LIFE

BY

NATHAN DRISKELL MA, LPC–S, NCC

COPYRIGHT

Nathan Driskell MA, LPC-S, NCC
17510 Huffmeister Rd. Suite #103
Cypress, TX 77429
https://nathandriskell.com

TABLE OF CONTENTS

INTRODUCTION

Before we begin the next 30 days together, I have a question to ask. Why are you reading this book? Take a moment to answer, and be honest. Are you reading this book because your parent/boss/significant other wants you to? Are you reading this book because others have told you you're an addict? **Have you made the choice to change?**

If you are reading this book to please others, understand you will fail. You can go through the motions, follow the activities, and finish the book. However, you will not fully understand yourself and your problem; you will struggle with your addiction and make little progress.

I know this sounds harsh, but it is reality. Your spouse, parents, friends, or therapist cannot control your addiction. You have to make the choice to change, or you will fail. If you want to change, you have a good chance of making progress. If deep down you are not ready to change, then progress will be slow or non-existent.

You may have told yourself the Internet is not addictive, therefore, you cannot have a problem. Everything and anything can be addictive. The mental health community is slow to admitting the addictive nature of the Internet and electronics because of a lack of research. The Internet can be more addictive than drugs and alcohol, as I have seen this addiction first hand.

How would I know this? Because like you, I am an Internet addict. Besides being a therapist, I am a gaming addict. I spent six years of my life trapped in an online game. During this time I ignored family, friends, and risked my future, all in the service of addiction.

Even though I quit the game years ago, I continue to have urges to play. That game and many others are at my fingertips 24 hours a day, seven days a week. I could binge in a game at any time. Having my own business I could take off of work with no consequence. No boss or parent can force me to stop. Every day, I control if I work, or if I binge.

So, what makes this book unique, and how can it help you? The difference between this book and others is my personal experiences with gaming and electronics addiction. I have an understanding of the thoughts, the lies, and the behaviors that come with being addicted to the Internet. I also have experience treating the addiction, as in my private practice I specialize in treating Internet and gaming addiction. I know both perspectives: the addict and the specialist. This book will present you with both sides of the issue, in an attempt to help you take back control of your life.

Understand this will be a difficult experience. I am going to ask you to make radical changes in your life. You will be limiting access to electronics. You will be creating daily routines you will begin to follow for the rest of your life. You will be going out in public and meeting people, learning how to interact in the real world.

Each day you will have activities to perform. These activities are required to continue through the book. Some will be easy; some will be extremely difficult. One of the goals of this book is to learn who you are. The first 3rd of this book focuses on who you are as a person, how your addiction has affected you. This knowledge will help you find your purpose, which is critical in helping you fight your addiction. In therapy, I often have my Clients undergo these same activities.

Speaking of therapists, I recommend you have one while working through this book. This book is NOT designed to replace therapy! Therapy is a critical process for anyone who is an addict. This book should be used in conjunction with therapy, as a therapist can help you work through parts of this book for maximum effect. Even if the therapist does not specialize in treating Internet addiction, as long as the therapist understands addictions, they will work.

At times this book may feel somewhat personal, as I often refer to myself and the struggles I had to face. I feel these segments are important so you can see how I experienced my addiction and the actions I perform to manage it.

To that end, I should introduce myself. My name is Nathan Driskell, and I am a therapist in the Houston / Cypress area. I have been a therapist for over six years, and throughout most of this time, I have specialized in treating Internet / Gaming Addiction. I am a nerd, having grown up with computers, and have experience as a web designer and network administrator. I understand technology and have worked in the public and private sector. While I no longer work in computers, I continue to keep up with the latest technologies. As far as computers, games, and the Internet in general, I enjoy them as a hobby.

It is time for us to begin our journey together. Be warned, I am sometimes blunt as I do not believe in wasting time. Therefore each chapter is short and to the point. Most chapters take 5-10 minutes to read. Once you have finished reading a chapter, complete the activity assigned. Some activities are quick; some may take hours. You will need to be committed to complete this book, as hours of work will go into it. Have faith in yourself, as you can do this.

I have divided this book into three parts: Insight, Action, and Maintenance. Insight focuses on who you are, how your addiction has affected you, and what you want for your future. Action includes all the changes you will make in your daily life, such as limiting access to the Internet & changing how you think. Maintenance concludes the book with completing your final daily routines, as well as setting goals for your long term future.

Let us begin our journey together. Onward to Day 1!

PART 1: INSIGHT

DAY 1: ACCEPTANCE & PREPARATION

Today's activity will be one of the most difficult you will complete in this book. It will also be one of the most important. Your first task is to fully accept that you are an addict and that you need help.

On the surface, this sounds simple. You can say, "Yes, I am an addict, and I need help," and leave it at that. You can mouth the words and skip to Day 2. You can choose to work through this book, to please another, while inside deciding not to change. Or you can choose to fully accept you have a problem and decide it is time to make changes in your life.

It is time to accept you are an addict and that your past ways of dealing with your addiction have failed. It may have cost you your relationship. It may have cost you your job. It may have cost you your health. Whatever it has cost you, it is going to continue to cost until you decide to change. No matter the addiction, may it be the Internet, drugs, or alcohol, accepting the addiction is the first step to recovery and control.

It took me six years to accept I needed help for my addiction. My addiction to computer games began when I was a senior in high school. Back in the late 90's, I began to play an online game with around 40,000 players. At the time it was state of the art and offered a real, dynamic world. I quickly rose to power in the game and made many friends. For the next six years, I would spend 12-14 hours a day in this world. I had friends, money, power, and respect. I felt my life had meaning, that I was someone special. Even though it was just a game, for me, it was my life.

I learned to multitask during my college years, dividing my time between class and gaming. I often did both at the same time. I made good grades, and even though I had few real life friends, I had enough in-game friends to be satisfied.

I refused to see myself as an addict, for I did not want to quit. I would justify my addiction by saying, "addicts are losers who live under a bridge," or "I cannot be an addict, I make good grades in school." My biggest lie was: "I have spent 5-6 years playing, I have put too much time in it to quit!". Do any of these lies sound familiar?

For me, acceptance of my addiction occurred in my 5th year of college. I was having a rough time in the game, and one day it finally dawned on me that I was an addict. In the past, I ignored my friends and family as they tried to convince me to quit. In one moment I fully understood I was an addict, and I could not continue living my life the way I had. It was if my whole world changed in an instant. I decided that day I had to take drastic action to kick my addiction.

I knew I needed to distance myself from the game and everyone who played it. I gave my accounts to my best friend in the game with instructions to never give them back. I cut ties with all my friends in the game and told them I would never speak to them again. I knew, for me, if I were near anyone who played the game, I would relapse. I had to burn my bridges and walk away.

It was the most difficult decision I have ever made. The pain I felt when I was done, with no game, no friends, and no life, was almost unbearable. I remember feeling like a complete loser and failure, with nothing to show for my life. For the next few days, I grieved my loss, then choose to get up and make a new life.

I took my computer knowledge learned while playing the game and became a Web Designer. I became employed with my University and started to talk more to people. By the time I graduated, I had replaced the game with real life friends and a sense of purpose. I believe my choice to quit the game saved my life, and has allowed me to write this book so I can help you save yours.

Do not give into the temptation to beat yourself up and think you are a failure for being an addict. Acceptance is not condemnation. You do not need to hate yourself for you to accept you have a problem. Yes, you could have done things differently to avoid the addiction, but the past is the past, and you cannot change it. Excessive guilt is your enemy and is a thought type you will learn to combat while working through this book.

Today's Activities

First, you are going to create a binder you will use while you complete the activities in this book. This binder will contain the insights you will learn about yourself and will be vital continuing forward. To complete the binder you will need the following materials:

- One 3-Ring Binder (Size does not matter).
- One 3-Ring Hole Punch.

- A Computer with a Printer.

You most likely have these items lying around your house. Create the binder now and be ready to use it starting tomorrow. Keep this binder once you finish this book, as you can refer to it in times of crisis.

For your next activity, I want you to make a list of the difficulties acceptance will pose for you. Acceptance is a difficult task for anyone, as we have to be true to ourselves and see things we do not wish to. This list can have as few as three items or as many as 50. Below are examples of why acceptance would be difficult:

- I do not want to accept I am an addict because I do not want to change.

- I am afraid I do not know how to change or cannot maintain it.
- Without the Internet, I have nothing else to do, and I would not know how to cope.
- Accepting I am an addict means I am broken or a failure.
- People will judge me and think I am a failure if I accept I am an addict.
- If I accept I am an addict, I can never change.
- I do not want to be labeled an addict, and accepting I am an addict is a label.

- Everyone else is an Internet addict, why should I accept it if others will not?

Listing your struggles with acceptance will give you insight into the hold your addiction has on you. The more you know about your addiction, the better able you are to fight it. Most of the items in the list above were my own as I refused to accept my addiction for years.

Your list should not include things people have told you about yourself or your addiction. These are your thoughts, your fears. You have to be real with yourself, and this list is a beginning. Create your list, and be honest, as you never have to share it with anyone.

Quick To-Do List

1. Create a Binder to use while working this book.

2. Make a list of reasons why accepting you are an Internet addict will be difficult, keeping in mind this is your list, and be honest.

Tomorrow's Focus

Tomorrow you will continue to focus on the fears you have about yourself as well as learning more about who you are as a person. You will be examining your life, from your strengths, weaknesses, and motivations. You will begin to create a picture as of who you are, and who you want to be in the future. The first part of this book will be mostly about learning more about yourself and your addiction, so you can see how it has impacted your life. Learning who you are is a critical step in learning to control your addiction.

DAY 2: WHO ARE YOU?

In Day 1, we discussed accepting your addiction, which was most likely unpleasant. For most of us, it is difficult to face ourselves, as we often try to hide the truth. By beginning the process of accepting your addiction, you are in a better place to combat it. To better combat your addiction, you need a better understanding of who you are as a person.

When was the last time you were asked: "Who are you?". For most of us, it was a question we were asked as children. As adults, we rarely think about who we are or where we have been. While "who are you?" is a simple question, it is difficult to answer. We have no basis for comparison as to what a good answer would be. More importantly, if no one knows what a good answer is, then why ask the question?

Asking this question is important; as it helps you learn more about yourself. You are more than an addiction; you are a person with hopes, dreams, successes and failures. You are complex with great qualities and devastating weaknesses. For you to beat your addiction, you need to know where you have been in life, and where you want to go. Without direction, your addiction will likely continue.

What makes up a good answer? A good answer involves your strengths, weaknesses, desires and motivations. It is real, with no fluff or filler. It is not something to make you feel good. Often answering this question is a painful experience, so much so I have watched people cry answering it. If you are emotional while answering this question, you have done it correctly.

A good answer is raw and honest, with no pretense or flattery. You are not trying to impress anyone or get away with something. An honest, real answer about your life is critical to understanding yourself. Your answer is unique and does not have to look like mine. Below is my personal example:

"Who am I as a person? I am a flawed, addicted mess. I have numerous addictions. I am addicted to games, electronics, sugar, being lazy. I am a procrastinator. I am often sarcastic and can be a jerk. For most of my life, I have hated myself and felt I was trash. I often wonder if I am a hypocrite, as I try to help people with addictions when I am also an addict. I sometimes think I help no one and have wasted my life.

For years I would look in the mirror and hate what I saw. My mind often tells me I can do no right. Even when I have successes in my life, my mind laughs at them and says I could have done better. I am always at war with myself, and sometimes I get tired of trying.

But, even though I feel these things, I know they are lies. I am addicted to being negative and beating myself up. I have succeeded in many things. I have helped hundreds of people. I have saved lives. I am smart, caring and do try to do the right thing. Sometimes I fail, and when I do, I have to fight from beating myself up. I am respected, and people care about me. Even in these things, I have to fight being negative, as it is my nature.

I am not content. I want more. I want a bigger practice. I want to speak across the country. I want to be more in control of my life. I need control. It's why my addictions exist. It is a form of control in my life because in the past I felt I had none.

So even though I have to fight with being negative, fight with my addictions, I know I will win. I have gone this far, and I will not stop. I will get past the loathing, the hatred, and will not let my addictions stop me. I have too many people depending on me now, and because of them, and myself, I will succeed. It will be hard, but I will succeed".

Above is a small sample of my answer. Notice the weakness I discuss, from my addiction to games, to my sarcastic nature. A good answer discusses multiple weaknesses and issues. Not every problem in your life is because of your addiction! Also notice the feelings I express, as feelings and emotions are important parts of your answer.

While most of my answer appeared dark and negative, it did not end that way. I ended discussing my strengths, as well as my goals and plans for the future. End your answer on a positive note, as you want to come away from the exercise feeling optimistic and hopeful. Begin your answer with who you are in the past, and end with who you want to be in the future.

Today's Activities

You are going to answer this question in a paper around 1-2 pages. You will be honest with yourself and put time and thought into it. No one needs to read this paper, as it is just for you. If you are seeing a therapist, this paper would be good to share, but this is your choice.

Be 100% honest with yourself and pour it out on the page. Do not worry about spelling or grammar. Focus only on the truth. Most of my Clients who have completed this task write 3-5 pages. By completing this exercise, you will have more insight as to who you are and how your addiction has influenced your thinking. Dig deep, and do not be afraid to write down things that are painful. By choosing to read this book, you will need to face painful memories of the past.

If you need help beginning the paper, look back to the list you made on Day 1 on accepting your addiction. These items can help you begin writing about yourself and how the addiction has affected you. Once your paper is complete, print it out and put it in your binder. You will refer to it as we continue.

Quick To-Do List

1. Write a 1–2 page paper answering the question, "Who are you?". In this paper, you will be honest with yourself and focus on your strengths, weaknesses, addictions, and future.

Tomorrow's Focus

You may feel emotionally drained once you have completed your paper. If so, this is normal, do not judge yourself on how you feel. Take a break for the rest of the day, so you are ready for tomorrow's task. Tomorrow you are going to look at the strengths you mentioned in this paper, and expand on them. Your strengths will pave the way to the future, as they will help you determine your purpose.

DAY 3: STRENGTHS

If I were to ask you to make a list of weaknesses, how difficult would it be? For many, it would be an easy task. Your failings and faults would likely flow from you without much effort. Would the same be true if you were to list your strengths?

For many, thinking about, much less listing their strengths would be difficult. It is often considered prideful to mention our strengths. Somehow, being honest with ourselves over our positive traits has turned into a sin.

For you to overcome your addiction, you need to know where your strengths lie. If you think you have none, stop and be honest with yourself. Often addicts are self-critical and beat themselves up. They feel they should be strong enough to beat their addiction, and when they fail they heap more guilt and blame.

The truth is, you have strengths. Everyone has them. These strengths will become sources of motivation and will keep you from relapse. They will help you in finding your purpose in life and giving you a sense of direction.

What would be a good example of strengths? I will again be your guinea pig as I give a list of what I consider some of my strengths. Your list will, and should, be different from mine. At the end of this chapter, you will be making your own.

My Strengths (In No Set Order)

- Intelligent – I am good at figuring out problems and learning new information.
- Educated – I have completed undergraduate, graduate school, and have spent hundreds of hours in study and research in my career.
- Scholarly – Through my education and study I have learned how to study and research and can teach myself new skills.
- Focused – When I work, I am often highly focused and can get tasks done while ignoring distractions.
- Healthy – I am in good health and have no major health problems that can get in the way of my happiness.
- Good Listener – I can listen to lengthy conversations and can keep focus, as well as provide insights into the conversations.
- Good Working Memory – I can remember much of the things that happen in my life without the need for lists or schedules, which allows me to focus all my attention on my Clients.
- Well-Read – I have read hundreds of books for entertainment, education, and self-improvement.

The above list is a small sample of what your list could contain. Below are more examples you can use while making your list:

Accurate	Generous
Adventurous	Good Looking
Ambitious	Independent
Analytical	Kind
Artistic	Leader
Athletic	Logical
Brave	Motivated
Caring	Orderly
Clever	Outgoing
Compassionate	Patient
Confident	Respectful
Creative	Serious
Dedicated	Spiritual
Entertaining	Straightforward
Fair	Tactful
Friendly	Warm

Today's Activities

Today you are going to make your list of your strengths. I want you to make a list of at least ten strengths. I want you to spend at least 30 minutes while making this list. Like mine, I want you to describe what your strengths mean to you. Your list will include words not on the list above. Be creative with it. This list will be used later to in helping you find your purpose.

Be sure to include strengths only you consider. Do not list what your mother or your friends think are strengths. This list is your own. Be honest with it, without self-loathing or condemnation.

For some, this may be a difficult activity. It is easy to dismiss ourselves and feel we are worthless. Often negative thoughts keep us in ruts. If you feel you cannot do this activity, stop for a time then come back to it. By focusing on your strengths, your perception of yourself will begin to change.

Quick To-Do List

1. Make a list of at least ten strengths, describing each strength as it applies to you. Be honest with this list, and make it your own. Print out this list and add it to your binder.

Tomorrow's Focus

Tomorrow, you will begin the process of finding your purpose, which will depend on the list you create today. Your strengths will help to point out possible careers you can begin to research. Working on creating a positive, healthy future will give your addiction less of a foothold in your life.

DAY 4: FINDING YOUR PURPOSE

Now that you have completed your list of strengths, you have a more realistic picture of yourself. What themes did you notice with your strengths? Your list begins the process of finding a purpose for the rest of your life, as our strengths can point us in the right direction.

What is the first thing that pops to mind when you think of the word purpose? For some, career and job aspirations come to mind. For others, they view purpose as the reason they are alive. This reason can include family obligations and social concerns. Both answers are correct, as your purpose is what defines you as a person and shapes your actions.

The problem is, finding a purpose is not something you just stumble across. You need to spend time and energy discovering it. Some people have known their purpose from a young age. They knew what they wanted and stuck with it. However, most people struggle with finding a purpose and often miss their chance at finding it.

I have found a lack of purpose to be a contributing factor for many of my Internet addicted Clients. For most, they have no idea what they want for their future beyond playing video games or being on social media. They often enter college at the request of their parents, only to drop out soon after. They are afraid of the future and do not know their place in the world. Their parents have no idea how to solve the problem and have often banned all access to electronics. The addiction continues, and the problem remains unsolved.

If this sounds familiar, know you are not alone. Fear of the future is a real concern that is becoming more common. Finding your purpose in the world is a daunting task that will take time and work. Below are three steps that can help you find your purpose.

1: Patience

The first step is to relax and give it time. You do not need to choose today what the rest of your life will hold. You need time to think about your options. If you are a teenager or a young adult, this is one of the reasons the first two years of college are general classes. Taking various classes can expose you to different ideas.

If you are an adult in the workforce, do not despair. One's purpose can change in different times of their life. Your purpose when you are 30 may not be the same as when you are 50. It is not uncommon for adults to decide to exit their careers. If this is you, consider your options over time. You may not need to exit your career, but change your activities within it.

For the next few months, while you are at work or school, take note on where your thoughts drift when you are idle. Do you sometimes imagine you are in a different job? Do you sometimes daydream about a life where you are doing something exciting or challenging? Sometimes these thoughts are ways our minds communicate with us, giving us suggestions on what to do next. Some of these thoughts will be fantasies that are not realistic. Ignore those and focus on the ones you could achieve. In this process, your mind will often give you reasons why you cannot do a specific job or career. Fear is your enemy, and you need to fight it.

2: Fight the Fear

Many people do not find their purpose due to fear. It is easy to convince yourself of what you cannot do as opposed to what you can. We tell ourselves that we are not smart enough, not motivated enough, or just not good enough to accomplish our goals. We give excuses, such as we do not have the time, or it would cost too much, or that others may judge us for our choices.

Fear often leads to excuses. Many of my Clients have told me they cannot complete college because it takes too long, or that they are not smart enough. Many tell me they do not have the drive or motivation to become successful. Why then do they have the drive and motivation to spend 12 hours playing a game? Because motivation is a choice, they have chosen to be motivated by video games.

If motivation is a choice, then we all can choose to be motivated about our future. If we sit and think about all the reasons why we could fail, we will not try. Instead, think about all the ways you can succeed and what you would want to do with your success.

Do understand, you are going to have fears while you are finding your purpose. Everyone has fears of what could happen, or if we are good enough. People who are successful acknowledge their fears then work to combat them. If you feel your purpose is to be a doctor, and you are afraid of it being difficult, this is a rational fear. If you let your fears be excuses to quit, then you are letting fear win.

3: You're Purpose Will Change

At the beginning of life's journey, your destination will change the more time you spend traveling. You will become a different person as you work through your purpose, and your outlook will change. A career you thought would last you through your life may become stagnant and dull. It is common for people to change careers later in life.

Many of my Internet addicted Clients are afraid of choosing the wrong career and are afraid of making the wrong choice. They have seen their parents or other family members make mistakes, and are afraid they will do the same. They avoid choosing a career, instead focusing on something unrealistic, like becoming a YouTube star or a professional gamer. They use this fear as fuel for their addiction, as a form of justification.

Even if you decide on a purpose, you may change your mind at a later date. You are not a failure if you change your mind later. Nothing is a failure if we choose to learn from it. Combat the fear over making an incorrect choice and begin to consider your options.

Today's Activity

Today, you are going to make a list of careers that interest you. From this list, you can begin to chart a purpose. This list will include at least three possible career choices you would like to investigate. Do not focus on the difficulty of these careers or the amount of education or time it would take to become successful in them. Any career you choose will take time and work to become successful.

For each career on your list, you need to provide reasons as to why this career is appealing. List these reasons with the career. These reasons, or motivators, are what you will gain from the career. Some possibilities include money, flexibility, challenge, security, specific interests, etc. If you have problems finding these motivators, you need to look into a different career. Your list of strengths from yesterday will help you in this process.

Your list may have three careers, or it may have more. Make sure this list is yours, not what others suggest. To find a purpose, you have to focus on what you want, not what others expect from you. No one list looks alike.

Spend some time while making this list, do not rush it. This list can and will change over time, so do not worry about changing your mind later. This list will help you narrow down your career choices. If you have a career or know your purpose already, instead write about what motivates you in your career and where you would like to go next within it.

Quick To-Do List

1. Make a list of at least three careers you find interesting, including motivators for each career. If you already have a career, then write down what you would like next in your career.

Tomorrow's Focus

By creating your list of possible careers and your motivators for them, you can begin to get an idea of what you want for your future. Tomorrow will begin to focus specifically on your addiction, as you will begin to face the consequences. Your addiction has robbed you of being happy and has sabotaged your future. You are going to face these consequences, so you fully understand what is at stake.

DAY 5: CONSEQUENCES OF YOUR ADDICTION

By now, hopefully, you have accepted you are an addict and desire to make changes in your life. You are at this point in your life for a reason. Your addiction is out of control, and you are tired of it. You have made the choice to change, and while others can influence your choice, you are the one in charge.

You have spent the first part of this book learning more about you. You have more knowledge about yourself now than when you began. It is time to use this knowledge to change. But first, you need to accept the damage your addiction has done, not just to you, but to others.

Your addiction to the Internet has most likely caused damage to your relationships. Your job or schooling has most likely suffered. Your mental and physical health may also be in decline. We are going to look into each of these areas, so you can get a better idea what your addiction has cost you.

Relationship Damage

Ask yourself, how many times have you refused to do something social, instead choosing to be online? Maybe your parents wanted you to watch something on television, but you were too busy playing an online game. Maybe you're significant other wanted to go to a movie but you would rather be watching YouTube. Maybe you went to the movie or watched television, but were looking at your phone the entire time and did not pay attention to anything.

If you are honest, this is likely all the time. The people in our lives want us to be a part of them, but we are refusing due to our smartphones or computers. When was the last time you went to a restaurant and did not spend part of the meal on your phone? Our neglect of others is doing damage to our relationships, but we do not see it.

We are losing our ability to have real, meaningful conversations. How often do you look at your phone while having a conversation? In our society, it is becoming acceptable to speak and use our phones at the same time. Over time, however, those closest to us may tire of our neglect and move on. It is ironic how the Internet connects us to thousands of anonymous people, but at the same time, disconnects us from those who matter.

No relationship lasts forever. The question is, how long will your relationships last if you do not learn to control your addiction?

Career / School Damage

If you are a student, how are your grades? If you are employed, when was your last raise? Did you fail any classes this year? Did you lose your job? While being addicted to the Internet, your performance has likely suffered. It is hard to be successful if you are on your phone, or are obsessing on your addiction.

As a society, most of us are becoming addicted to our smartphones. We use them hundreds of times a day in almost any environment. As it has become more acceptable, it is easy to justify our addiction. If most people have a problem, and they don't have to change, then why do I? We lie to ourselves and justify our addiction because we do not want to change. Our smartphones have distracted us from living life.

While working to find your purpose and manage your life, you do not have time for distractions. You need to be motivated and focused. Some online time is fine, but if it is distracting you from living your life, then you need to change. It will take countless hours of work and effort to become successful. Successful people do not have time to be addicted to their phones or the Internet.

Physical Health / Mental Health Damage

Are you overweight? You most likely are. How can I generalize that? Most Internet addicts sit most of the day on their computers or phones and rarely gain physical exercise. Add in the awful diets most of us have, it is no wonder many of us are overweight. As someone who is overweight, at times I struggle to live a healthy lifestyle.

A sedentary lifestyle leads to high blood pressure, heart disease and a host of other problems. For a non-addict, it is difficult to maintain a healthy lifestyle. It is nearly impossible for an addict, as there is not enough time to partake in healthy activities.

Addiction often takes a toll on mental health. Depression and anxiety are common with addictions, including Internet addiction. Many of my Internet addicted Clients have social anxiety and have turned to the Internet as a coping skill. I have never treated a case of Internet Addiction that did not involve another problem.

Your addiction has affected your health to a great degree. Be mindful of this, and let it be a motivator. Your activity for today is to list the consequence of your Internet addiction in your relationships, career, and health.

Today's Activity

You are going to make a list covering all the consequences of your addiction. You need to break your list into the three areas covered above. For each area, list the consequences you have noticed in your life.

Be specific with your list. While it may be painful, it is required as you need to understand the cost you have paid for your addiction. Even though this may be difficult, understand that controlling your addiction will improve all three areas.

You cannot change the past, and some of these consequences are not fixable. If your addiction has caused the end of a relationship, you cannot change it. What you can do is learn from these consequences, and then work to improve yourself. From making this list, you will see what areas in your life you need to improve and begin to make goals to fix them.

Quick To-Do List

1. Make a list of the consequences of your addiction, divided into the following categories: relationships, school/career, and physical/mental health. List all consequence, past and present.

Tomorrow's Focus

Once you complete your list, you will be more motivated to make changes in your life. The next four days will be critical, as you are going to begin to make a list of all activities you conduct online. You will note the websites you visit, the games you play, and the social media apps you use. You will create a digital footprint of your online life, so you can see what activities take up the most of your time. It is time to learn how much time your addiction is stealing from your life.

DAY 6: YOUR DIGITAL FOOTPRINT, PART 1 – ACCESS

Your addiction to the Internet has cost you greatly. Yesterday taught you how much damage it has done in your life. Now, you are going to begin learning how much time you spend online, and what fuels your addiction.

The next four days will focus on your online habits, with the first focusing on the devices you use to connect to the Internet. You are going to make a list of all devices, from cell phones to tablets to computers you use.

Access = Gateway Drug

Knowing what electronics you use to give yourself access to the Internet is critical, as you are going to make changes to how you use these devices.

Most people use many different electronic devices to access the Internet. It can be gaming counsels such as the Playstation 4, the Xbox One, or the Wii U. It may be tablets, such as iPads or Samsung Tabs. It could be Portable gaming counsels such as the Nintendo DS. It could be the Oculus Rift or the HTC Vive, the first big names in virtual reality technology for PC.

In the days to follow you will be tracking how much time you spend online on each device, as well as what activities you conduct. You are going to make a digital snapshot of your online life. You will begin to see just how much time you spend online, as well as the activities you conduct. Creating a digital footprint sounds simple, but in reality, it is not. The next few days will take work on your part, as you're going to keep a logbook on you to write down your online activities.

Today's Activity

You are going to make a list of every device you use to access the Internet. You will then rank the devices in order of most use. Be through and think about how you access the Internet. Do you use a work PC? Include it. Do you use your brother's DS? Include it. Complete this list and include it in your binder. The devices at the top of your list will be the ones you will need to pay special attention to as you work through this book.

Quick To-Do List

1. Make a list of all devices you use online, and order them from greatest usage. Print out this list and put it in your binder.

Tomorrow's Focus

With your list complete, you will begin to monitor your Internet usage. The next two days you will record all your time online. Do not deviate from your normal routine, as you need to see a true picture. Only by seeing yourself and your activities for what they are you will see just how impactful your addiction is. Once this list is complete, you will begin to make changes in your life.

DAY 7 & 8: YOUR DIGITAL FOOTPRINT, PART 2 – CATALOGING

It is time to begin cataloging your time online. For the next two days, you are going to note everything you do online. From how much time you spend opening an e-mail, to how long you are on Twitter, to how much time you are on Snapchat. You will record all time spent on non-work or school activities.

The goal is to be specific. You need to list every website, every social media application, every game you play. You need a realistic picture of how much time you spend on every application, as you most likely have no idea as to how much time you spend. Once you complete these two days, you will be shocked to discover how much time you are online.

The question is, how will you record all your time online? You have two options. You can carry a logbook and manually record your time, which will prove difficult. Or you can use an application for your smartphone, tablet, or computer to aid you in the process.

No matter what you choose, you will need to log some your online activities manually. There is no one program that will log all your time across all your devices. Being as thorough as possible is the goal, so you can see a realistic picture of how much time you spend with electronics.

If you have an Android phone or have a PC, Mac, or Linux system, the best program to use is called RescueTime. If you have an iPhone or any device that uses iOS, you can keep track of how much time you spend on applications via system settings.

What is RescueTime?

RescueTime is an application that sits in the background of your phone or PC that collects data on the programs you use. It sets timers for each application or website you visit. It logs how much time you spend and then puts this information in an easy to use graph format. For example, if you are using Twitter on your PC, it would log how much time you spend on it each day, as well as any other websites or applications you use.

The great thing about RescueTime is the lack of user interaction. You do not need to start and stop timers, like other timing applications. You can install the program, set it up, then go about your day without needing to remember to start or stop a timer.

Not only does RescueTime collect data, but you can also set goals and even tell it to limit your access to certain websites or applications. For example, you can tell RescueTime to limit access to social media apps like Facebook or Snapchat, and it will not permit access until you allow it.

If you have a PC, Mac, Android Phone or Linux OS, then install RescueTime on all devices you use. For this book, we will assume you have installed RescueTime, as you will use it beyond this chapter. I recommend the Premium version, which will give you a 14-day free trial. This version is $9.00 a month, and for the rest of this book, you will need it. $9.00 is a small price to pay for a program that can help you change your life. I recommend you continue to use RescueTime beyond this book, so you are more aware of how you spend your time.

RescueTime Link: https://www.rescuetime.com/

Note: If you work with sensitive data, like classified data or HIPAA, then you cannot use RescueTime, as they store information about your activities. While they only store document names or website addresses, this could include sensitive information. For this reason, I could not test RescueTime myself, as I work with sensitive data.

What if I have an iPhone or an iPad?

Unfortunately, if you have an iPhone, iPad, or any device that use iOS, then RescueTime will not work. Something within iOS prohibits automatic recording needed for RescueTime to function. There are no alternatives that will automatically record the applications or websites you visit on iOS.

Fortunately, if you have iOS 9 or above, you can check within system settings to find how much time you have spent in each application. To find this information: click the following:

'Settings' than 'Battery' then tap the clock icon on at the top right of the screen.

Your applications are listed in order from greatest to least time used. It will also tell you how much time each application has run in the background but ignore this. Do not focus on system related activities such as Home and Lock Screen, only focus on applications you use. On some versions of iOS, you can check the past eight hours, 24 hours, and even seven days.

The downside of this is there is no specific information on each activity. For example, Safari, iOS's browser, will not list each website viewed. It will give an overall amount of time, but you have no idea of how much time you have spent on each website.

Also, there is no graph-based interface and no way to compare your time day to day. You will have to create a log and record your time daily. There is no getting round it, as there are no automatic tracking applications for iOS.

Today's Activity

Determine if you can use RescueTime, and if so, install it on all supported devices. You will not be able to install these applications on all devices you own, as in game counsels and iPads. However, the more devices you can monitor, the better picture you will get about your online activities.

If you cannot install RescueTime, then you need to log how much time you spend on each application or website you visit. Remembering to log each website and application will be difficult, and you will likely forget at times. Your log will not be perfect, but the more accurate, the better overall picture you will have on your digital life.

Even if you have RescueTime, it will not help you record your time for gaming systems, Windows Phones, or other devices. You will need to add this information in RescueTime manually.

If you cannot use RescueTime, or have no devices that support it, you can log your time via the logbook I have included at my website. The logbook is a Microsoft Excel document, with each tab corresponding to a day. The logbook is divided into categories such as gaming, social media, gambling, pornography and other. The logbook will automatically calculate the hours for each category. Visit my website to download the logbook:

Logbook Link: http://nathandriskell.com/internet-addiction-kicking-habit/logbook.xlsx

These next two days will likely be difficult and tedious. You may feel the urge to give up, feeling this is a waste of time. These thoughts are normal. Push through them and continue to catalog your time.

Quick To-Do List

1. Install RescueTime on all supported devices.
2. Monitor all online activity, including non-supported devices, as accurately as possible. Add this time in RescueTime or the log provided in this chapter.

Tomorrow's Focus

At the end of the next two days, you will gain insight into your digital life. While two days is not a large sample, it is a snapshot of time that can give you an idea of how much time you spend online. Once you have finished the next two days, you will analyze this data to determine what applications you use most. Later, you will determine **why** you engage in these activities, to see what fuels your addiction.

DAY 9: YOUR DIGITAL FOOTPRINT, PART 3 – ANALYSIS

Now that you have spent the past two days cataloging your digital life, what did you find? Did you spend as much time online as you thought? Were your activities what you expected? Most likely you underestimated your online presence, and now you should have a better understanding on how much time your addiction is costing you.

Time is something you cannot buy, nor ever get back. Many of the hours you have spent online were a waste of time that you cannot afford to lose. While we all need hobbies, your addiction goes beyond a hobby, and it has cost you precious time.

Today's Activity

For today's activity, you are going to make a list of the most time-consuming activities you have conducted within the past two days. For this list, exclude any school, work, or meaningful activities that benefit you. Include the top five activities that are time wasters, such as games, social media, pornography, etc. For each item, put an average of how much time you spend on it daily by adding up the time you spent for both days and dividing by 2.

Once this list is complete, you will know what activities you need to reduce from your life. If you spend 8 hours a day in social media, then this will be an area to reduce. If you spend 10 hours a day in an online game, this needs to change.

There is a good chance the top activities on your list will not surprise you. What may be surprising is how much time you spend on them.

If you can use RescueTime, then you are going to continue to track your online usage while working through this book. Seeing how much time you spend can tell you if the changes you have made are working. You need to keep RescueTime installed and running on all supported devices, and each day input the other online activities that are not automatically cataloged, such as game counsels. If you cannot use RescueTime, continue to log your activity in the log you completed yesterday.

Quick To-Do List

1. Make a list of the five applications or websites that accounted for the most time spent the past two days. Add up the times for both days and divide by 2 to gain an average. Include the average with your list.
2. Continue to log your online activities daily by using your logbook or RescueTime.

Tomorrow's Focus

You now know how much time you spend online as well as what applications and websites are the most problematic. You are learning just how much time your addiction is costing you, and due to your work in this book, know the damage it has done to your relationships, career, and health. Tomorrow, you will begin to learn the answer as to **why** you are addicted, by discovering what these applications do for you. Once you know why you are addicted, you can begin to make changes in your life.

DAY 10 & 11: NEEDS

Now that you know how much time you spend with specific activities, the question is **why** you spend this time. The question of why is critical, as you need to understand what drives your addiction. If you do not answer why something is addictive, you will be doomed to repeat it.

To answer this question, you need to understand what you gain from your addiction. Everything we do as humans we do for a reason. While some actions can be random, overall we make choices on what we do. Even if something harms us, there is a benefit, at least in the short term.

For example, take someone who is an alcoholic. Everyone knows drinking to excess is damaging and destructive. While there may be short-term benefits, long-term consequences can be devastating. If the alcoholic knows this, why does he drink? He knows he is damaging his life, his relationships with others, and will eventually lose everything. He drinks because he gains a short-term benefit. It may be too dull a pain he has experienced in the past. It may be to feel more social. Whatever the reason, he drinks because he gains a short term benefit he does not know how to fulfill by other means.

Therefore, everything we do helps us in the short-term, even if it harms us in the long term. Remember this quote, as it is a reason why you are addicted to the Internet. Your online activities are providing you with a benefit, one that has become an addiction. The question is, what needs to you gain from them?

What are Needs?

A need is something we require as a person to feel complete. Everyone has needs, which can include physical constructs such as food, shelter, safety, etc. Needs can also include relationships, the search for meaning, relaxation, and affection. Needs are the basis of human existence. We exist to fulfill these needs and will spend most of our lives in the pursuit of them.

While many of our needs overlap, everyone has unique needs. If I were to make a list of needs and compare it with yours, our lists would be different. We all have different value systems, each just as unique as our needs. Addictions often form to fulfill a need, even if it is destructive.

When I spent six years addicted to an online game, my needs for this game included self-esteem, control, power, and connection. In the game, I was one of the most powerful players. I spent much of my time becoming more powerful so I could feel better about myself. The game supplied my need for connection, as I had many friends, in contrast to my real life. The game supplied my needs for control and power, as I knew how to win, and felt more powerful than most of my peers. Because I was powerful and well known, my self-esteem improved. The game supplied my needs, even though the game was not real. In my mind, the game was more important than real life, and I did not care how my needs were met.

For me to quit the game, I had to understand what I gained from it. By knowing self-esteem was an issue, I started to change how I thought about myself. By gaining more confidence in myself, I was able to gain more control over my life. This control lead to power, as I felt in charge of my life. Once I quit the game, I focused on real world alternatives to supply my needs.

List of Needs

Below is a list of needs grouped by a common theme. You will use this list to determine the needs your addiction supplies. You can choose as many needs as you feel relate to you and your addiction.

Connection	Connection (Continued)
Acceptance	Mutuality
Affection	Nurturing
Appreciation	Respect
Belonging	Self-Respect
Cooperation	Safety
Communication	Security

Closeness	Stability
Community	Support
Companionship	To Know
Consideration	To See
Consistency	To Understand
Empathy	Trust
Inclusion	Warmth
Intimacy	Love

Physical

Air

Food

Exercise

Sleep

Sex

Safety

Shelter

Touch

Water

Honesty

Authenticity

Integrity

Presence

Play

Peace

Joy

Humor

Beauty

Communion

Ease

Equality

Harmony

Inspiration

Order

Autonomy

Choice

Freedom

Independence

Space

Spontaneity

Meaning

Awareness

Challenge

Clarity

Competence

Consciousness

Contribution

Creativity

Discovery

Efficacy

Effectiveness

Growth

Hope

Learning

Mourning

Participation

Purpose

Stimulation

Understanding

This list was created by the Center for Nonviolent Communication:
© 2005 by Center for Nonviolent Communication
Website: www.cnvc.org   cnvc@cnvc.org
Phone: +1.505-244-4041

This list is a sample; there are many more needs than these. If your need is not on this list, list it regardless.

Today's Activity

For the next two days, you are going to notice what needs exist while you are online. As you play an online game, be mindful of what you are feeling. Do you feel powerful when you win? While on social media, do you feel as if your opinions matter? Do you feel connected with others? Do you feel creative, or do you like discovering new ideas? Every application you use, website you visit or game you play satisfies a need.

Once these two days are complete, take your list from yesterday and add in all the needs you discovered. Each application may have one need or five, depending on you and your experiences. If a need is not in the list above, add your own.

Do not rush through each application looking for a need. Use the application as normal, noting how you feel. Let this be a natural process. Once finished, look at the needs list, and see what matches your experience.

Quick To-Do List

1. For the next two days, note the needs for each activity in your top 5 list yesterday and then at the end of tomorrow, list the needs to each item.

Tomorrow's Focus

Now that you have made your list of needs, it is time to begin to find alternatives to the Internet to fulfill them. In my experience, many of the needs people choose are relationship based. The best way to combat your addiction is to improve upon real world relationships. Tomorrow you will begin the process of making real world relationships. You are going to go outside your comfort zone, but if you are serious about controlling your addiction, you will attempt it.

DAY 12: RELATIONSHIPS

There is a good chance some of the needs you found yesterday included relationships with others. It is common for many to use the Internet as a way to socialize. With the popularity of social media, the Internet is the main way people keep in contact with one another. The problem with the Internet is it can lead to fake relationships.

As most social media networks rely on followers or "friends," we sometimes feel those we connect with care about us. We post pictures, stories, "updates" about our lives, and when we get a "thumbs up" or a "like," we feel as if these people care. The more "likes" we get, the more important and connected we feel. In the moment, these people may have "liked" your update, however, they likely do not care about you unless you have spent time forging a real relationship.

How can a stranger you have never met, who is a friend of a friend, have an emotional connection to you? With hundreds of connections, you do not have time to make real relationships, no matter how much time you spend online. Real relationships take more time and attention to create then social media allows. While it is possible to develop real relationships online, most are only acquaintances.

It is time to create new relationships, new friendships. It is time to make them in real life. Before you do so, however, it is best to learn what separates a real friend from an acquaintance.

What is a Real Friend?

A real friend is someone who you have spent time with, in which you can be yourself with no games or pretense. You are not afraid to open up and discuss private matters. A real friend is someone who cares about you and wants the best for you. Sometimes, a real friend sacrifices their happiness for you and vice versa.

A real friend would go at 3:00 AM to pick you up off the side of the road, even if they had a job interview the following morning. A real friend would give you money if you needed it, without question, because they trust you enough to pay them back. A real friend takes time to listen to your problems and is there to help you. A real friend expects all these in return.

From the definition above, how many real friends do you have? There is a good chance you have none. If you have 1-2 real friends, you have done well. I have two friends whom I trust, whom I consider real friends. I have known them each for almost 20 years. I spend time with them, playing games, going out to eat, talking about life. I trust them and have no reservations.

It is difficult to make a real friend, which is why most people don't have one. It is risky, as you have to open yourself to another, and sometimes you will get hurt. But when you find a real friend, spending time with them will be more fulfilling than spending time online.

The point of today's topic is to show you what you are missing from the relationships in your life. You are most likely lonely, and the Internet is a way to dull this feeling. If you have many "friends" online, you can trick your mind into not feeling lonely. While you can make friendships with people online, it will never be the same as a real life relationship.

Today's activity will require you to take a step outside your online relationships. You are going to use the Internet to find real-life groups of people, where within the next two weeks you will be meeting in real life, to begin creating new relationships.

Today's Activity

Today, you are going to go to the website www.meetup.com, where you are going to find a group to join. While it sounds like a dating site, it is a collection of real-life groups in your area. Often these groups meet once or twice a month in a public place, like a mall or a library. The great thing about meetup.com is it is free service where you can even create a group. Here is a sample of some of the main categories:

Arts & Culture	Movements & Politics
Book Clubs	Movies & Film
Career & Business	Music
Cars & Motorcycles	Spirituality
Dancing	Paranormal
Education & Learning	Parents & Family
Fashion & Beauty	Religion
Fitness	Sci-Fi & Fantasy
Food & Drink	Singles
Games	Socializing
Health & Wellbeing	Sports
Hobbies & Crafts	Tech

Each category will have numerous groups to join. You can search for specific interests or browse each category. Follow the instructions below to sign up:

1. Go to https://www.meetup.com.
2. Click the Sign Up button on the upper right side of the page.
3. You can use your Facebook or Google account to sign up, or you can use your e-mail address. If choosing to sign up with an e-mail address,

select your city. In any case, enter your name and e-mail address and click the Signup button.

4. If signing up via e-mail, meetup.com will send a confirmation e-mail. Follow the instructions in it to confirm your account. You would skip this step if you used your Facebook or Google account.

5. Meetup.com will ask for your photo, generated from Facebook or Google. You can upload a photo, or skip this step.

6. Next, a list of 24 interests will pop up. Select as many as apply to you then click the Next button.

7. You will now narrow down your interests. Check the ones you are most interested in and click Next.

8. A list of groups near you will appear. Click on them to read a description. Click the Plus button on the groups you find interesting. You choose to leave any groups later if you wish. Click the Next link in the upper right of the page when done.

9. You can invite friends to meetup.com if you wish. However, you can skip this step.

10. A list of groups in your area will appear with specific events in the next few weeks. Look through this list and choose any groups you find appealing. RSVP to events you find interesting. Some events are first come first serve, so RSVP to reserve your spot.

Look through the list of groups and choose two events to attend in the next two weeks. Make sure you choose events you are interested in, even if they involve online activities. The goal is to go out and meet new people, so you can feel more comfortable in interacting with others. The more people you meet, the greater the chance you will make friends. As you work through this book you will be exploring new hobbies, and in turn, more meetup groups to join. Check back often to see new events from your groups, or to search for new groups.

Quick To-Do List

1. Join meetup.com, choose at least two different groups to join and RSVP to at least two events within the next two weeks.

Tomorrow's Focus

For many, today's activity will prove difficult. It is common for Internet addicts to have social anxiety. The Internet allows for safe, convenient communication not found in person. Asking someone with social anxiety to go out in public and meet a group of total strangers is a big step.

Learning healthy coping skills can help manage social anxiety. For many, the Internet is a coping skill, as it helps distract from life's pain. In this book, you will learn coping skills needed to manage your life and combat your addiction. Tomorrow, your learning begins.

DAY 13: HEALTHY COPING SKILLS

As we are nearing the midpoint of our journey into controlling your addiction, it is time to begin to learn healthy coping skills to manage the anxiety and lack of stimulation you will face. Tomorrow you will begin to limit your access to electronics, so today's activities will be critical.

Today you are going to learn three different coping skills that will help you improve mood and manage anxiety. Coping skills are just that, skills you use over time that will help you. Coping skills need practice before they can provide the maximum effect. Therefore, each of these coping skills will be used daily for now on. Over time they will help you to manage your anxiety and improve how you feel.

Grounding

The first coping skill you will learn is grounding. Grounding is one of the few coping skills you can practice anywhere. It is quick, convenient, and powerful. I have seen grounding work for Clients with ADHD, PTSD, Schizophrenia, Depression and Addiction. Grounding is one of the most powerful coping skills you can learn.

What is grounding? Grounding involves using the five senses to focus on what is happening at the moment. We often get caught up in one feeling at a time, while ignoring what our bodies tell us. If we are craving stimulation, say from an online game, we may ignore how tired we are, or our body temperature, or physical pain. Grounding helps tune into what our bodies are telling us, as well as a breaking point for our focus. For example, if I have a craving to play an online game, then use a grounding technique, I have distracted myself from the craving, giving my mind time to find an alternative.

To use a grounding technique, you will use all five senses to describe the world around you. The technique has a set order and method you need to memorize. It is quite simple and should be easy to memorize after the first few times. For each sense, you are going to describe different sensations provided by it. For example, you will describe five objects you see. For each object, you will describe the characteristics of the object. The more detail you provide, the better. Below is an example:

Object: a box fan

"I see a fan. It has a square shape, but the corners are round. It is white with its blades spinning quickly. There is a grill over the fan with slats for the air to come out. On top of the fan is a gray knob you turn to adjust the fan's speed. The fan has a white handle on top."

I could have said "I see a white fan," but this is not enough detail. The more effort you put into the description, the better grounding will work.

You will begin with five things you see, followed by four things you feel. Next, you will describe three things you hear, followed by two things you smell. You will end with one thing you taste. The order and amount of objects do not change.

Sight

Focus on objects you see in your environment. The objects themselves do not matter, as long as they are real, physical objects. Good examples are paintings, furniture, plants, dishes, papers and electronics. Describe them in detail to yourself. You do not need to speak out loud; you can think these descriptions. The power of grounding is its portability. No one needs to know you are doing it. Below is another example of how I would describe an object:

Object: a small digital picture frame

"I see a digital picture frame. The frame portion is black, and overall it is a rectangle. It is maybe 7 inches across. The picture changes every 10 seconds, and the screen is backlit. A black cord extends from the picture frame to the wall. Each picture is different, mostly from nature or museums I have visited in the past".

The description above gives a good mental picture of the picture frame. The more time you focus on your descriptions, the better you will be at distracting from a craving or a moment of anxiety. Describe five different objects in your environment in a similar manner.

Feel

You will now describe how you feel in four different areas. These include physical sensations, such as hunger, pain, temperature, and feelings, such as anxious, sad, or happy. It is best to try to get a mix of feelings, so you know how your body feels physically as well as emotionally. Below is an example of an internal feeling:

Internal feeling: Anxiety

"I feel somewhat anxious right now. I feel this because I am about to speak in front of a group, and I am afraid of how it will go. This anxiety feels like butterflies in my stomach, and my foot is tapping as a way to distract myself from it".

In the example above, anxiety was the feeling over speaking in front of a group. The cause, speaking in front of a group, lead to the feeling of anxiety. A physical sensation of butterflies in the stomach preceded the feeling. The foot tapping was interesting, as it could be a small coping skill designed to lessen the anxiety. Let your emotional feelings look like this example if possible.

Below is an example of a physical feeling:

Physical feeling: Hot

"I feel hot right now due to the heat in my office. It is around 100 degrees outside, and my air conditioner is not up to the task. I feel sweet on my back and stomach, and I feel wet all over. It is an annoying feeling I do not like".

In this example, the physical feeling, hot, was caused by the outside temperature and an underpowered air conditioner. Physical sensations such as feeling sweet on the stomach and wetness describe more feelings. This example also included a response to this physical sensation, the feeling of annoyance. By knowing this feeling, actions can be taken to lessen the annoyance, such as getting a glass of water. Let your example follow this format. Now, describe four things you feel, with a mix of internal and external feelings.

Hear

Next, turn to the sounds you hear in the environment. This one may prove more difficult as we often discount background noise. You may need to sit quietly for a few moments and focus on the sounds around you. Below is an example:

"I hear the noise maker outside my office door. It is a consistent sound, and it is slightly loud. The sound is of static used to drawn out sounds from within my office. It is easy to ignore".

In this example, the source of the noise was mentioned, as well as how loud it was. The last portion, easy to ignore, describes how important the sound is. Most of the sounds you hear will be background sounds you will easily dismiss. Knowing they are there, however, gives you more awareness of your surroundings, and distracts you from yourself. Go ahead and focus on three sounds you hear near you, describing as I have above.

Smell

The further down the list we go, the more focus it takes to describe our senses. As most of our senses produce only background information, it takes more mental energy to focus. It may prove difficult to distinguish two different smells, as we often blend them together in our mind. Below is an example of two different smells:

Smells: Pine & Ketchup

"I smell a sort of cleaning agent, something with pine. It is a faint smell that I did not notice unless I focus. There is another smell in the room; I think it is of ketchup. It is a tangy smell but extremely faint as if it was present hours

ago. The pine smell is easier to distinguish, but the ketchup smell is present if I focus. I do not like the combination of the smells together, but I can ignore it as both smells are slight".

Notice how I describe how the smells work together, as well as how strong they are. I noted how I felt about the smells, which is good as part of this exercise is to note your feelings. I described the possible sources for the smells, even though I was not completely sure. Go ahead and describe two smells you smell right now.

Taste

The last sense, taste, may be easy or difficult depending on how long it has been since you had something to eat or drink. Taste and smell are linked, and something you described for smell may also be present in taste. If this is the case, focus on a different taste, as we often can taste more than one thing at a time. Below is an example:

Taste example: mint

"I taste a mint I had around 2 hours ago before I left for my office. It is a slight flavor that has decreased over time. It is a pleasant flavor that takes the place of the pasta I had for lunch. It is fading and will not last much longer".

I noted the taste, the possible source of the taste, as well as what I thought about it. I also included how long I believe the taste will last. Go ahead and try for yourself.

Once you have completed all five senses, ask yourself how you feel, and what you want to focus on next. The point of the grounding exercise is to distract yourself from the negative feeling or urge you are experiencing. Focus on something you need to do, then take steps to complete it. If you still feel this urge, repeat the grounding exercise until you feel more in control. Grounding takes time to practice and get right. You will not be an expert in a week.

Equal Breathing (Deep Breathing Exercise)

Everyone knows how to breathe, but did you know we often do it wrong? We often breathe in one breath for a second or two, then exhale and repeat. We often do not get enough oxygen in our bodies, stressing our brains. Learning how to control your breathing will help reduce stress and improve your overall functioning.

While there are numerous deep breathing exercises, you will learn the easiest and most accessible. Equal breathing is a simple exercise you can use anywhere, just like grounding. You can do it in the car, at your desk at work, or in public. To perform an equal breathing exercise, do the following:

1. Notice your natural breath, and calmly take note on how long each breath takes.
2. Take one breath and count to four, holding the breath. Note how you feel when you reach four.
3. Exhale slowly, counting to four. Note how you feel when your breath is empty.

4. Repeat steps 2-3 for 5-10 minutes, making sure your inhales and exhales are around the same length.

Over time you can increase the count if you wish. The more you practice, the longer you will be able to hold your breath without distraction. At first, it will be difficult to match your breaths without complete focus, but over time it will become more natural. After years of practice, some people can breathe this way automatically.

Like grounding, practice equal breathing often. Use it when stressed or before something unpleasant. Equal breathing also works well before bed, and if you cannot sleep. Combining equal breathing and meditation is recommended. Speaking of meditation...

Meditation

Meditation has gotten a bad rap as something with mats and silly poses. Meditation, in the terms I will describe, is an activity where you clear your mind of thoughts and expectations. I used to think Meditation was pointless until I experienced it firsthand.

Meditation is the act of clearing your mind in a controlled manner. You can use guided meditation, where an instructor is giving you instructions or affirmations. You can use musical meditation, where you listen to soothing sounds to help clear your mind. The key is repeating this behavior daily for at least two months until it forms into a habit.

In the beginning, it will be difficult to clear your mind, as you have had little practice doing so. We are often undisciplined with our thoughts, and allow ourselves to get swept up in them. Meditation is learning to control your thoughts. The more practice, the easier it becomes to block out intrusive thoughts. As you become less dependent on the Internet, you are going to need a way to control intrusive thoughts, as they will lead to urges and binges. Meditating during urges is a great way to resolve them.

Below is a list of free online resources that can help you meditate. Some, like Pandora, have meditation channels which sometimes have advertisements. Try the different channels and determine what works for you:

- Pandora: Online music service. Search for Meditation and try the different channels: http://www.pandora.com/
- Spotify: Online music service. Search for Meditation or Guided Meditation channels. https://www.spotify.com/

- YouTube: Video playing service. Search for Guided Meditation or Meditation music. https://www.youtube.com/

Today's Activity

Today, you are going to begin to develop a meditation routine, as well as practice grounding and equal breathing. For the next three days, pick a time of the day you can meditate for 15 minutes. During your meditation period, you will be alone, with no distractions. You can choose to use calming music, to use a guided meditation exercise, or to use the music of your choice. The style of meditation is not important, the habit you form is. Later in this book, you will incorporate meditation into your daily routine.

As you meditate, focus on the music or instructions you hear. Do not focus on your problems, your tasks, or your day. Focus on those thoughts later and allow yourself to relax. It may be tempting to sleep during meditation, but sleep is not the goal. Keep yourself focused on the music you hear, and let yourself drift from thoughts about yourself. Equal breathing while meditating will help keep you focused and enhance the experience.

Each day you will also practice the grounding and equal breathing exercises you learned above. Grounding and equal breathing are perfect for moments where you feel anxious or distracted. Try to practice both at least ten times a day, until they become easy. You will use grounding and equal breathing to help calm down later while you are slowly reducing your online time.

Quick To-Do List

1. Begin to meditate daily by choosing a time where you will not be distracted, then spend 15 minutes listening to music or guided meditation, while focusing on the music, not yourself or your responsibilities.
2. Practice grounding and equal breathing at least ten times a day, during times you need to calm down, or gain focus.

Tomorrow's Focus

You have reached the end of Part 1 of this book. You have gained insight into yourself and your addiction and have learned healthy coping skills. Next, you will begin changing your behaviors to limit your time online. During this process you may feel lost, bored and urges may be frequent. Tomorrow you will begin to limit access to the Internet, bit by bit until you have a more balanced life. Have confidence in yourself, as you will learn how to manage your addiction. It is time to begin making changes in your daily life.

PART 2: ACTION

DAY 14: YOUR DAILY ROUTINE – SLEEP

It is time to begin making changes that will make it easier to manage your addiction to the Internet. To begin this process, you need to create a daily routine that over time will be healthy but easy to follow. The first part of this routine is your wake/sleep schedule.

The Importance of Sleep

Sleep is critical to your ability to manage your addiction, as sleep influences your overall health. Most addicts do not get enough sleep, due to binging into the early hours of the morning. For people who are addicted to the Internet, healthy sleep is often rare.

My gaming addiction caused massive damage to my sleep schedule that continues to this day. In my quest to become more powerful, my character was in the game 24 hours a day, doing activities on a script. When it was time for me to sleep, I would run the script, and have it alert me if I needed to do something in the game. On average I woke up 10-15 times a night, all to serve my addiction. Even though it has been years since I have done this, I still wake up five or so times a night for no reason. While I have fixed my sleep schedule, the damage remains.

Many Internet addicts wake up often to get online or to check a status update. For children, this is extremely damaging as they need a full night's sleep. Access to phones and tablets at night is often too tempting to ignore. Easy access to electronics must be eliminated for healthy sleep to resume.

Removing Electronics From Your Bedroom

As phones, tablets, and computers have most likely become a distraction at night, it is time to remove them from your room. Remove all electronics from your bedroom, including televisions, computers, tablets, gaming consuls, portable gaming devices, and phones. Unplug your electronics, including your chargers, and move them to different rooms of the house. If you cannot do this, due to living in a one room apartment, charge your phone during the day, then turn it off at night and put it in a sealed container, such as a suitcase, to make it difficult to access.

For you to change, radical action is needed. I am not suggesting you sell or get rid of your electronics. However, you need to remove them from your bedroom. Other rooms of the house can have electronics, but your bedroom needs to be an electronics-free zone. By removing temptations to be on electronics at night, your sleep will improve.

Today's Activity

For today's activity, besides removing all electronics from your room, you are going to create a routine, a habit, of when you wake up in the morning and when you go to sleep. You need to make sure to get at least 8 hours of sleep, as you are most likely sleep deprived and may need more than average. You need to pick a time you go to sleep each night and a time you wake up each morning. For the rest of your time in this book, each day you are going to adhere to this routine. You are going to form a healthy sleeping habit that will last once this book is complete.

For example, if you choose 11:00 PM to go to sleep, you will wake up at 7:00 or 8:00 AM. You are going to follow this sleep schedule each day, even on weekends. You need to be sure to follow the schedule exactly until it becomes routine. You can pick the times you want that best works for your schedule, but whatever times you choose, you need to be consistent.

For this habit to work, you need to buy an alarm clock if you do not already have one. Many use their phone's alarm to wake themselves up. You are not going to use your phone anymore, as your phone will not be in your bedroom. Buy an old-fashioned alarm clock, one with no access to the Internet. Use your alarm clock daily to adjust to your new sleeping schedule.

Quick To-Do List

1. Remove all electronics from your room, especially phones, tablets, and computers. Make sure to remove all electronic chargers as well.
2. Create a new sleep schedule, making sure it is for 8-9 hours a night. Begin to follow this schedule daily as you work through this book.
3. Buy an alarm clock if you do not already have one, and use it daily while working this book.

Tomorrow's Focus

With your room free of electronics, you can now focus on getting restful sleep. Over time you will notice you have more energy during the day, and your mood may improve. Improving your sleep is an important first step, as tomorrow you are going to continue building a daily routine which will include less time online. Continue to practice your meditation, equal breathing and grounding techniques, as you will need them in the days ahead.

DAY 15: YOUR DAILY ROUTINE – MORNINGS & GOALS

How you begin your day is important for how productive you will be during it. As you are beginning to set a sleep/wake habit, your morning routine will be an important part of the process. The habits you build in the morning are key in helping you keep focus during the day.

As you have removed phones, tablets, or anything electronic from your room at night, you are free to begin your routine without distractions. Often most addicts spend the beginning of the morning checking their phone or playing a game. Instead, you are going to use healthy coping skills to begin your day.

Grounding & Equal Breathing Return

Remember the coping skills you learned earlier in the book? Hopefully, you are practicing them daily and are starting to see results. You are going to start each day with a grounding exercise. By completing the exercise, you will be more focused on your body, your environment, and your day. If you have been practicing grounding each day, this should be getting easier and quicker to complete.

For a quick recap, you will describe five things you see in detail, four things you feel (internally, as in emotions, and externally, as in temperature), three things you hear, two things you smell, and one thing you taste. Give as much detail as possible, as the more focus you include, the more the exercise works.

Once done with grounding, perform an equal breathing exercise. Calm your breathing, then take a breath and hold it for four seconds. Note how you feel once you reach four, then begin to exhale for four seconds. Repeat this pattern, making sure to inhale and exhale for the same length. Practice equal breathing for five to ten minutes.

Daily Goals

Each morning you are going to make a list of goals you want to complete for the day. These goals can include work goals, chores, home responsibilities, hobbies, and social relationships. You are going to make a plan for your day, one you will stick to as closely as possible. You will do this at the beginning of the day, so it is fresh and real in your mind. While it may be difficult to focus and think right after you wake up, the grounding exercise above should help you focus.

For example, here is a sample of goals I may set for myself in a day:

- I will complete two chapters in this book.
- I will see all my scheduled Clients.

- I will do notes and treatment plans for the Clients I saw yesterday.
- I will vacuum my room and my office area.
- I will watch the Basketball game later tonight.
- I will read a chapter in my new book.

Notice the words "I will"? You are promising you will complete these activities. These are not suggestions, but set goals you will complete. Notice how my list includes hobbies. While it may sound strange, setting time for hobbies is important, as downtime is important for mental and physical health. Make sure any hobbies you list are **not** online activities. The days I set specific goals are the days I do well.

Today's Activity

You are going to create a list, like the one above, of your goals for today. Make sure to include work goals, chores, social responsibilities, and hobbies. Be as specific as possible. While making this list, use a pen and paper, and take this list of goals with you throughout your day. I do not want you to use a computer or something electronic for creating this list, as you may be distracted. In time, once you have more control over your addiction, then you can use a phone or computer to make this list. It may take time, but it will be a good beginning to your day. Make sure to take this list with you, so you can check off your goals as you complete them.

Once the list is complete, finish your morning routine, such as breakfast, taking a shower, and other typical hygiene-related tasks.

Quick To-Do List

1. As you get up in the morning, complete a grounding and equal breathing exercise to help you wake up and gain focus.
2. Create a list of your daily goals, making sure to include work tasks, chores, social obligations and hobbies. Take this list with you and refer to it throughout the day.

Tomorrow's Focus

As you work on your morning routine, it will become easier to complete your list and keep focus on the important tasks in your life. Tomorrow will focus on your nightly routine, as there are steps you need to take to be sure you have a good evening. You will be limiting the electronics you use in the evenings, to reduce the overall stimulation you experience. Reducing this stimulation will help improve your sleep and health.

DAY 16: YOUR DAILY ROUTINE – EVENINGS

For the past two days, you have begun work on changing your daily routine. You have removed all electronics from your room. You have created a morning routine and are making daily goals. Now, you will work on your evening routine. How you end your day is just as important as how you begin it.

You most likely spend your evenings on your phone, tablet, gaming console or computer. You most likely play until you go to sleep, without doing anything else. Each night is likely the same with little variation. In the past, you most likely slept with your phone and tablet and checked it often throughout the night.

Now that you have removed all electronics from your room, this is not an issue. Now, you need to change what you do before you go to sleep. Meditating before you sleep is a great way to clear your mind.

Meditation Returns

There is a reason why I wanted you to learn about grounding and meditation before this chapter. I want you to become familiar with both, as you will use them daily. Meditation is the perfect activity to do before you go to sleep. It is great for clearing your mind, letting yourself fall asleep easier. Each night, right before you go to bed, you are going to spend 15 minutes meditating.

You can use music or guided meditation if you wish. Using your phone or tablet to provide the music is fine, as long as you remove the phone or tablet once finished. During the meditation, you will focus on the music or words as you actively avoid focus on yourself. Do not plan your day or worry about problems. You will meditate each night before you go to bed, and over time it will become easier to fall asleep.

A Trip To The Library or Bookstore

Do you like to read books? Regardless of the answer, reading is a vital activity as it helps with memory, vocabulary, and it can be very entertaining. I find reading to be an enjoyable part of my day. By reading, I do not mean reading something boring or instructional. I mean reading something fun that you enjoy.

You are going to be reading a book each night for at least a half hour. Reading helps the brain to unwind, putting you in a more relaxed state. To get this book, you are going to take a trip to the bookstore.

Why not just download and use an ebook like everyone else? Ebooks are electronic, and we are working to reduce your dependence on electronics. Also, reading a book on a screen is more stimulating than on paper, and we are trying to reduce your overall stimulation. While you may feel you are addicted to electronics and the Internet, in reality, you're addicted to stimulation. By reading a paper book, you are not as stimulated as if you were looking at a screen.

You may not be a reader and may feel like this activity is too difficult. There are millions of books to choose from, and in time you will find something you enjoy. Think about your favorite activities. What kind of books would match? You can look online for information on books and read book reviews if you wish, but do not buy an ebook or read online. Reading a book not only helps you relax, but it can also improve your vocabulary and reading skills.

Today's Activity

Today, find a bookstore or library and look for a book. I suggest three different books, in case you do not like the one you pick. A library is great as it costs nothing. Look online to find the location of a library or bookstore and pick up three books.

Some people who are addicted to electronics or the Internet have social anxiety that makes it difficult to go out in public. For them, going to a bookstore or a library may be extremely difficult. Going out in public is part of the process, as becoming more comfortable with being in public will indirectly reduce your dependence on the Internet. If this is a difficult task for you, have someone go with you for support. By going out in public, you are taking a step into the world, which while scary, will eventually be easier.

An hour before you go to bed, you will begin your nighttime routine. First, complete all hygiene related tasks, such as brushing your teeth. Next, pick one of the three books and begin reading. Try to limit your reading to 30 minutes, or a couple of chapters a night. Once you are done reading, meditate for 15 minutes. Once done, remove all electronic chargers from your room and go to sleep. You will repeat this exactly for the rest of your time with this book, and hopefully beyond.

Quick To-Do List

1. Go to a bookstore or library and pick up three different books. Pick books you would like to read, something that would hold your interest.
2. Begin your night time routine. An hour before you go to bed, complete all hygiene tasks, then read for about a half hour, followed by 15 minutes of meditation. Remove any electronic devices from your room and go to sleep.

Tomorrow's Focus

So far you have begun to make small changes in your life by developing a daily routine. You have removed all electronics from your room and have developed a sleep/wake schedule. Before we begin limiting your access to electronics during the day, a focus on social activities is required. Building a healthy social life will leave less time for electronics while providing you with real, healthy relationships. Tomorrow you will continue making plans to interact with others in the real world and get out of your comfort zone. While difficult, be patient and have faith in yourself.

DAY 17: SOCIAL INTERLUDE PART 1

While online, how often are you performing the same activities, over and over? If you play a game, how much time do you spend grinding for experience? If you are on social media, how many photos can you see in a day? Repetition can become stagnant and dull. Often we are online, repeating the same actions, all in the name of social interaction.

Playing games online and spending time in social media provides the illusion of social interaction. Someone posts a cool image on Instagram, and you comment on it. Others comment on your image. You play an online game with someone, and after you had beaten them, you feel like you spent time with them. In reality, all you did was interact with text or graphics on a screen.

Most likely, you are not having real, in-depth conversations with people. Just to be clear, yelling comments and trolling someone on social media are not in depth conversations. When was the last time you sat with someone in real life and talked about yourself, about them, and about how you feel? For some, they have never had a real, in-depth conversation with someone face to face.

It is time to change, so you can have real friendships and have real conversations. To do so, you are going to make an active effort in communicating with others.

To that event, today you are going to plan an outing with someone in the real world.

Remember Meetup.com?

Hopefully, you have found two groups on meetup.com and had RSVPed to at least two meetings. If you have not done so, do so today. If you have, attend these meetings when they come up and see how they go. Attending these groups may be one of the scariest activities I am asking you to do in this book. For me, it would be difficult to go to a place of strangers, feeling out of place and awkward. You can do this, and need to do this, to know you can beat your addiction. In truth, social anxiety may be one of the reasons for your addiction, and in combating the anxiety, the Internet has less hold over you.

Make Plans With Friends or Family

If you have friends or family, you are going to be setting up a time to get together with them. It is ok to do something you want to do, as long as it is something that does not involve electronics. Going to a friends house and playing Xbox is not ok. The goal is to do something with your friends and family, in the real world, where you both can be focused and present.

Going to a park, a restaurant, a sporting event are all good ideas. Seeing a concert, going to a mall, or go to a museum. Going to a movie also works, as long as you spend some time together talking about it after. The point is to spend time with them where you can talk and get to know them better.

It may be tempting to look at your phone the entire time. If you feel this could be a problem, leave your phone in the trunk of your car or the glove compartment. The world will get on just fine without you for an hour or two. If you do not have any real world friends, or do not have any family, then take effort in finding groups on meetup.com.

Today's Activity

Go ahead and contact a friend or a family member and set up a time and place to get together. It can be anything as long as you are not on electronics the majority of the time. Try to choose a friend or family member who will also not be on their phone the entire time.

While with them, focus on having fun and being in the moment. Try not to worry about the future, or about problems you have. If you feel anxiety, perform a grounding or equal breathing exercise.

Make sure you have joined at least two groups on meetup.com. Check in to make sure the meetings you have picked are still scheduled. Do not forget to complete your morning and evening routines, as we have covered in previous chapters. Also, make sure you are still keeping track of your time online, with Rescue Time or a similar application. You will need this information in the next chapter.

Quick To-Do List

1. Contact a friend or family member and schedule a time to get together. Make sure you pick a public activity, something you can do in the real world.
2. Check in at meetup.com to confirm your meetings for the two groups you have joined.

Tomorrow's Focus

Now that you are working to be more social, the true work begins. It is time to begin limiting the activities you conduct online and the amount of time you spend. You will need all the information you have gathered from Rescue Time, or your log, to help determine what activities you need to limit. Your coping skills will be vital during the next few days, as it will be difficult limiting your time online.

DAY 18: LIMITING ACCESS PART 1

Today is going to be a difficult day. I am not going to sugar coat it. Today, you are going to begin to limit your access to the Internet. The person who is going to hold you accountable for this is you.

In truth, no book, doctor, therapist, or parent can make someone do anything. If you want to binge on electronics nothing will stop you. You are the one who is going to do the hard work and the one who will judge if you have been successful. That work begins today.

Reviewing the Data

Days ago you were asked to monitor all your time online. You listed the five most time-consuming activities and averaged the times. Today, you will review RescueTime or the log you created, and determine of these applications are the same. If so, then you know the applications you will need to limit going forward. If not, adjust your list. During the remainder of this book, you will continue to monitor your time online, so you can know if the changes you make are working.

Your list of applications can include examples such as Twitter, Facebook, Snapchat or games, such as Farmville, Team Fortress 2, or League of Legends.

Once you have your list, you are going to limit access to the least time-consuming applications.

Cutting Access

You are going to remove activity #5 and #4 from all portable devices. For example, if Twitter and Facebook are #5 and #4 on your list, you will remove the applications from your phone, or you will disable them if you cannot delete them. You are no longer going to have access to these applications during your day. Remove them from all portable devices, such as tablets and phones.

I am not telling you to delete your accounts to these networks. The goal is to limit access until you are at home. While you are at work, school or in public, you will be more focused and have less temptation to binge.

When you are home and have completed all your goals, then you can spend two hours a day on electronics. In the days to come you will be creating a set time for electronics usage. During this period you can use these applications. Until then, try to limit your access to two hours a day, once you have completed all your daily goals.

Why Not Limit My Most Time-Consuming Activity?

It may make more sense to begin to limit the most time-consuming activity on your list. However, most likely this activity is your main addiction, and at this point, you would most likely fail.

If you spend 10 hours a day playing a particular game, then I ask you to limit to two hours a day, you will most likely fail or not even try. This step is most likely too extreme, too difficult. By choosing activities that are less addictive, it will become easier to limit your access. In time it will not be such a shock. Later, you will be limiting your main activity to two hours a day, but for now, we will begin with your bottom two activities.

Today's Activity

It is time to go to each portable device and remove your bottom two applications you have listed. You may experience high levels of anxiety in this. If you do, use a grounding technique. If that does not help, meditate to clear your mind first.

Make sure to delete the applications from ALL portable devices. Do not leave the applications on one device in case of "cravings." Refer to the list you made of all your devices to make sure you do not miss one. It is easy to justify our actions when we are addicts, and by leaving a back door, you will find ways to cheat.

I know this is difficult. You may have thoughts of quitting, of not going forward with this book. These thoughts are normal and expected. You CAN do this. You do not NEED any of these applications or activities to live. Be positive and have faith in yourself and your recovery. By deleting these applications, you are making a bold statement to yourself about what you want for your future: freedom.

Quick To-Do List

1. Determine the top most time-consuming activities you conduct on a daily basis, then order them from least time consuming to most.
2. Remove the bottom two activities on your list from all portable devices.
3. Limit yourself to these bottom two activities to two hours a day going forward.

Tomorrow's Focus

Today was the most difficult day yet. It will get more difficult the further we get in this book. Tomorrow, however, we are going to take a break from something difficult, as you are going to have a free day to enjoy yourself, as long as you remember to follow the rules already in place.

DAY 19: DAY OF REST

You have done well to make it this far. You have started to make real changes in your life. You know more about yourself and what you want for your future. Today, you are going to pick some real world activities you enjoy, and are going to do them.

Have Fun!

Today's task is simple: to enjoy yourself and have fun, while at the same time limiting your access to electronics. Having fun does not include spending the entire day playing video games, or spending it on social media. You need to do other activities you enjoy, such as going to a movie, going out to eat or something else that is social. You pick whatever you want and enjoy the day, you have earned it.

Just Remember...

Continue with everything you have learned in the book so far. Today is a test run of how you will live life with more control of electronics. Continue with your sleep/wake schedule and make sure to create daily goals in the morning. Work to limit acccss to electronics in the evenings to two hours a day, and try not to use the two applications you removed from your mobile devices yesterday. Use grounding techniques and equal breathing and make sure to meditate in the evening before bed.

Today's Activity

Have fun in the real world, even if this is outside your comfort zone. Try not to worry about yourself, your progress, or your addiction. Enjoy yourself!

Quick To-Do List

1. Go someplace in the real world and have fun, but be sure to follow all the tasks you have been completing daily.

Tomorrow's Focus

Hopefully, today was a break that helped you recharge and refocus. Tomorrow we continue to limit your access online, by cutting another online activity from your list. A good idea would be to check out more meetup.com groups in the mean time, to see if there are more groups to join. The more social you are, the easier this process will be, as you will have less time to spend online. You have done well so far, keep it up!

DAY 20: LIMITING ACCESS PART 2

Over the past two days, how difficult was it without the two applications you removed from your mobile devices? You may have had some feelings of anxiety, especially if these applications were social. If you feel anxiety during any period, a grounding exercise will help you calm down and keep focus.

Today, you are going to continue to limit your applications. This time, you are going to remove the 3rd most used application on your list from all mobile devices. Also, you are also going to limit when you use your phone during the day.

Your Phone is Distracting You From Life

Answer this: do you browse your phone when you are eating? How about while you are driving? How about when you are watching a television program or having a conversation with a coworker? Most likely, the answer to most of these questions is yes.

It is not just you; it is all of us. I have to watch my phone usage and sometimes find it difficult not to check my phone in the middle of a conversation, or when I am driving down the freeway. The problem is, we are so used to this behavior we no longer notice when we do it.

The problem, again, is with communication and social relationships. If you are on your phone during a conversation, you are telling the person you are speaking with that they are not worth your undivided attention.

Take Control of your Phone

You're going to begin to take notice of when you check your phone and when you keep it away. Below is a list of places where you will keep your phone in your pocket, purse or someplace out of sight:

- While eating, especially out in public with people.
- While you are walking down the street.
- While in a shopping mall, store, or another retail establishment.
- While you drive.
- While at work (unless you use your phone for work).
- While at school (unless you use your phone for school).

In each location, keep your phone out of sight and focus on the environment. Use the phone only if needed. Addiction aside, many people are hurt or killed by not paying attention to their surroundings by being on their phones. While this may seem like common sense, most people use their phones in public and put themselves at risk of being robbed or hurt.

Today's Activity

Today, you will go to each portable device and delete your 3rd most used application. Make sure to delete this application from all portable devices, not just your cell phone. You can access this application from your computer within the two hours a day you have for social media or games.

Also, you will keep your cell phone out of sight while you are in public, by keeping your phone in a purse, pocket, or bag. While you are driving, I suggest you keep your phone in the trunk or glove compartment, especially if you are prone to check your phone while you drive. You can be out of touch with the world for awhile. It is not worth getting killed or killing someone else. Keeping all phones out of reach is a good way for families to talk and communicate with each other.

Don't forget to use your coping skills, as anxiety may be high. Keep up meditating at least once a day, as well as using grounding exercise when you have high levels of anxiety.

Quick To-Do List

1. Remove your 3rd most used application from your portable devices, giving yourself access to your computer during your two-hour window per day.
2. While in public, or driving, or eating, keep your cell phone out of sight, so you can begin to control your usage.

Tomorrow's Focus

Tomorrow, you are going to do something different that I hope will become a daily habit. You are going to begin to journal about your experiences while working this book. In the journal you will discuss the thoughts and urges you have had, and how you have managed them. This journal will be private and yours alone. Have a good rest of your day, and do not forget to follow your daily routine!

DAY 21: JOURNALING

As you are approaching the end of this book, it is important to begin cataloging your experiences. You most likely have had a rough journey, as the changes asked of you are difficult. You may have experienced more anxiety than normal. Today, you will begin the process of journaling, so you have a record of your thoughts and experiences. This journal will be a reference point when you look back at your experiences with this book.

Fortunately, journaling is not a complicated activity. A useful journal is one that is brief, honest, and completed often. You are writing this journal for yourself, designed for you to read and learn from at a later date. You have nothing to prove, and no one else should ever read it. Journaling is a private experience you only share with yourself. Journaling is a form of release and is a way to get out feelings or thoughts you cannot otherwise.

Journaling: An Example

So, what makes a good journal entry? Below is a sample journal entry if I was working through this book:

"August 5th, 2016

Today was rough. I began my day with my daily routine, which was to get my work done and to limit my time playing games. I started well and got most of my work done. I got distracted at times and one point gamed for an hour in the middle of the day. I get so bored in the afternoon, and my work can seem to drag on!

I got most of my work goals completed, but not as much as I wanted. Towards the end of the day, I quit work and binged on games for four hours. I did not read my book or socialize much. I feel like I failed today and that I will never get over this. I did better yesterday and do not know why today sucked as much as it did.

I will do better tomorrow. I will complete the work I did not finish today, and I will socialize more. I see friends tomorrow evening, and I plan to leave my phone in my car through most of it. Tomorrow will be better, I hope."

The overall theme of this entry is honesty. In it, the writer feels like they failed as they binged in a game and did not complete all their goals. Real feelings were discussed, with a focus on feelings of failure. Not all journal entries will be positive or happy. The point of a journal is to face your feelings and release them in a controlled way. For much of the entry above, the author felt like a failure as he did not accomplish his goals.

Toward the end, however, notice the undercurrent of hope. There was no beating up, no giving in. Anytime you complete a journal entry end on a positive note and do not leave broken down and defeated. Above, the writer feels they failed today, but they have a plan on how they will do better tomorrow. Use this format as the structure for your journal entry. I want you to list your accomplishments, your failures, and your plans on how you will eventually succeed.

Today's Activity

Today, begin your journal writing exercise. I want you to write about 1-2 paragraphs a day. Do not focus on grammar or spelling, as this is for your eyes only. Be honest about today and write about your experiences. Include problems you had at work, or school, or with people. Discuss your feelings and reactions to these problems. If you have had urges or gave into them, write it down. The main point of journaling is for you to be honest with yourself, and to release what you have experienced. Journaling is a powerful exercise in letting go of past feelings and regrets. I want you to journal every day for now on, even once you have finished this book.

Quick To-Do List

1. Begin a daily journal, and keep writing in it daily. Print it out and put it in your binder so you can refer to it in the future.

Tomorrow's Focus

Tomorrow, you will begin to work to limit your online access to two hours a day. These two hours are for entertainment purposes and do not include school or work. You are going to make a set time in the evening where you can be online. The rest of your time, if you are not working or studying you will be doing other activities. Hopefully, you are becoming more social and have attended a couple of meetup.com groups, as you are going to have more free time than you are used to. Have a good rest of your day, and let the journaling begin!

DAY 22: LIMITING ONLINE ACCESS TO 2 HOURS DAILY

It may be surprising to learn three weeks have gone by from the beginning of this journey. Has it seemed that long? Or has it felt longer? You are beginning to learn how to balance your time online and your time in the real world. Today, we are going to go one step father and focus on limiting your online time to two hours a day.

Work / School / Life Balance

It may be impossible to limit all your online time due to work or school demands. Limiting of time does not apply to school, work, research, or any productive activity in your life. The goal is to balance of your time online. The time you want to limit is your time on social media, playing games, and chatting with people. You have already limited your time in your bottom three most used applications to two hours a day. Now, you will create a set time each day for your two hours of online time. This two-hour window includes computers, television, phones, laptops, and gaming consoles.

Offline Hobbies

You may be thinking, "what the heck am I going to do for the rest of the evening if I cannot be online or watch TV?". Well, it is time to consider non-electronic hobbies. I know this sounds ancient and old school, but there are many different hobbies. Here is a list of possible hobbies you should consider:

- Reading a physical book.
- Taking a walk.
- Joining a gym / Developing an exercise routine.
- Playing sports, such as Basketball.
- Painting, drawing, etc.
- Listening to music (as long as you are NOT looking at a screen while listening).
- Listening to the radio (same principle as listening to music).
- Arts and Crafts.
- Going to a bookstore.
- Going to a mall, park, or another social event.
- Playing a musical instrument.
- Talking to friends on the phone.
- Meeting friends in real life.

- Studying another language or a subject you find interesting.

The list above is just a small list of possible hobbies you could do. If you spend time, you can think of more. Try out some on this list, and make your own. As long as you are not spending much of the time looking at a screen, it is acceptable. Use your phone to call a friend, or text them directions, or make plans. Do NOT spend 2-3 hours texting your friend instead of calling.

The point is to find other activities that enrich your life. Imagine a time before the Internet. What did people do for entertainment besides television? Most did many of the activities above. Some might seem corny, but people who have multiple hobbies have an easier task of balancing their life.

Today's Activity

Today, you will set a time of the day you will be allowed to use electronics for entertainment purposes. Make sure the time is the same for each day, so it is easier to become a habit. For example, if you get home at 5:00 PM, 7:00 PM until 9:00 PM would be a good time, once you have finished making dinner and cleaning up. Once 9:00 PM comes, turn off the electronics and find a hobby.

Hopefully, you have already made a trip to the library or bookstore and have some books to read. Read a half-hour, then prepare yourself to go to sleep. You do not need to do the same hobbies each day. Mix it up and try different things. Some days you may want to forgo your electronics time because you are out in public, for a meetup.com group or time with friends. One rule you MUST follow: electronic time does NOT carry over to the next day. If you are out with friends and miss your two hours, you cannot use those two hours tomorrow. You do not need to get back in the habit of binging, and four hours or more a day will set you back.

Make a list of hobbies you find interesting. Once done, print out this list and put it in your binder. If these are new hobbies, try them out for a time. If you do not like them, find others. The more hobbies you try, the more varied and balanced your life will become.

Quick To-Do List

1. Set a two hour period daily for you to be on electronics for fun. Each day, try to use electronics only at this time. Time does NOT carry over to the next day if not used!
2. Create a list of hobbies that do not involve electronics. Try to include at least four hobbies on your list. Begin these hobbies for the remainder of this book, and if they do not work, try others.

Tomorrow's Focus

Enjoy creating your list of hobbies. Over time you can find happiness if many different activities, even if they are not online. Tomorrow, you will continue to limit your access by removing another application from your phone. Soon your phone and other mobile devices will be limited, allowing you to focus on what is important, living life and having relationships. Continue to attend meetings via meetup.com and try to schedule time with friends. Have a good rest of your day, and continue your routines.

DAY 23: LIMITING ACCESS PART 3

With one week left, we have much to cover before you can take what you have learned and turn them into daily habits. Your goal is to continue these habits until they become second nature. Today, you are going to remove access to the second most time-consuming application from your phone and mobile devices.

A Recap

Hopefully, you have removed the bottom three applications from your list already. If you have not, do so today. These applications are time wasters that are distracting you from your life and responsibilities. You can use these applications during your two hours a day allotted for entertainment, but throughout your day, you need to focus on work, school, and relationships.

If your list did not include applications on your phone or tablet, make sure you limit them during your time at home. Often computer games or video games can be addictive, even more so than a phone application. Limiting your time on these is just as critical as limiting your time on mobile games or social media. As a recovering addict I have to limit my access to games, or I will binge 4-8 hours at a time. To do so, I make sure I have a list of goals, via my daily routine. Creating a daily routine, as you did on day 15, will help you keep on task. If I do not have set goals, I will binge on games and waste my day. I do not have time to binge on games, and if you want to find your purpose and live life, either do you.

Today's Activity

Right now, go ahead and remove the second application on your list from all your mobile devices. As with the other's, it should not take long. You may be feeling more anxiety as you remove more used applications, as you probably use these applications often. At times during the day, you may feel anxiety when you look for the application and it is not there. Fight the urge to reinstall the application. If you have reinstalled an application, remove them again and continue. We all have moments of weakness, where we give into urges we know are not healthy. The question is, do we return to the path or give up? By reading this book, you have chosen not to give up. Remove these applications, and take pride in knowing you are taking control of your addiction and your life.

Quick To-Do List

1. Remove the 2nd application on your list from all mobile devices. If you have reinstalled applications from your list, remove these as well, and focus on the future.

Tomorrow's Focus

With today's task complete, you are creating long-lasting changes in your life. Phones and mobile devices are tools to make your life easier, not to control you and limit your experiences. Tomorrow, you will begin a two-day process where you will begin to take a look at your thoughts, and how to gain more control over them. Controlling your thoughts will be a difficult process that will take years to master. Tomorrow will begin a process that will help you not just manage your addiction but will allow you to manage your life better.

DAY 24: AUTOMATIC NEGATIVE THOUGHTS – PART 1

Today is an important day, as you will begin to learn more about what controls your thoughts and urges. Controlling your thoughts is not a simple task, as our thoughts are often chaotic and negative. For the next two days, you will learn what goes into our thoughts, and how we can better control them and our behaviors.

Are All Thoughts True?

How often do you think your brain lies to you? When a thought comes to mind, does it have to be true, or can it be an impulse? If our brains lie to us, then how do we know what is true? These are all good questions, as our brains are extremely complex. Your brain is completing thousands of actions a second, often without your knowledge or input.

The problem begins with conscious thought. As humans, we are wired to notice threats to our lives. In the past, if we are not on the lookout for danger, we would have been eaten or killed. As a result, our brains have adapted to look for danger in all forms. The more threats we seek, the greater chances of staying alive.

What do threats have to do with thoughts? Threats are often negative thoughts used to seek out problems. If we feel something is a threat, our anxiety levels will rise, which allows us to be more alert and able to act.

Negative thoughts, in a way, are a type of survival skill. Negative thoughts can help us be more alert and adaptive.

The problem is over time we rely on negative thoughts too much and begin to believe them as truth. Sometimes, our brains lie to us as a way to protect us from something unpleasant. If I have social anxiety and do not want to interact with others, my brain my lie to me and tell me everyone is not to be trusted. This lie protects me from pain, even though it is false. Our brains lie to us in an attempt to shelter us from painful experiences. Over time, however, these thoughts become poisonous and prevent us from living life.

Automatic Negative Thoughts

Everyone has negative thoughts. If someone tells you they never have negative thoughts, they are lying. Everyone has negative thoughts, often hundreds of times daily. The term, Automatic Negative Thoughts, is a way to explain our thoughts, and how they work. Automatic means, well, automatic. These thoughts come without choice.

You may be thinking, if automatic negative thoughts always happen, then I am doomed to failure. False! You cannot control negative thoughts from appearing in your mind, but you can control how you **respond** to them.

For example, if someone with social anxiety was thinking of going out in public, they may have the following thought: "Everyone is going to look at me and judge me!". This thought would be automatic, appearing in their mind. Now, they can choose to believe this thought, allowing it to influence their actions, or they can challenge the thought as false. At this point, they are in control and can choose to believe the thought as truth, or a lie. Most often, automatic negative thoughts are lies designed to limit our exposure to pain, while consequently, causing more pain in the future.

Different Types of Automatic Negative Thoughts

An easy way to remember automatic negative thoughts is to use the word ANTS. Like real life ants, automatic negative thoughts sting and come in groups. One negative thought often leads to many. I did not come up with the concept of ANTS, that honor belongs to Dr. Daniel G. Amen. To learn more about his work, check out his work once done with this chapter:

3 Quick Steps To Stop Negative Thinking Now: http://danielamenmd.com/3-quick-steps-to-stop-negative-thinking-now/

Below is a list of the ten most common ANTS. We will spend the next two days going over each of them so that you will be better prepared. Make no mistake, ANTS are your enemy, and to fight your enemy, you have to know them.

- All or Nothing Thinking – thinking in terms of black and white, extremes.
- Overgeneralization – using words such as "always" and "never" directed at yourself.
- Filtering – stripping the positives from a situation and focusing only on the negatives.
- Mind Reading – thinking you know the thoughts of another, when in reality you don't.
- Should Statements – using the word "should" in a way to limit personal responsibility.
- Magnification – thinking something is worse than it is.
- Guilt – punishing yourself for past mistakes, as excuses to continue your addiction.
- Labeling – using negative words to punish yourself and to keep yourself from success.
- Emotional reasoning – viewing emotions as fact.
- Predicting the future – thinking you know the outcome of a situation when in reality you don't.

There is some overlap with this list, as many of these thoughts lead to the others. If you have seen these before, know ANTS are also known as cognitive distortions, with are often challenged in therapy. A therapist who practices Cognitive Behavioral Therapy knows ANTS well and can help you challenge negative thoughts.

Today's Activity

Today, we are going to cover the first five ANTS on our list. Once done, you are going to write down an example of the most common thought you experience from each listed, in a personalized example. You will begin to notice when you have these thoughts; then you will learn how you can change them from negative to positive.

All or Nothing Thinking

With All or Nothing Thinking, often thoughts are extreme. Things are all good, or all bad, with no middle ground. This kind of thinking can leave one feeling depressed and angry. Anytime something happens that is even slightly negative, it is completely bad, with no compromise.

For example, say your best friend did not show up for your birthday party. Your other friends and family did, and it was a good day overall. Well, it would have been a good day if you did not obsess over your friend's absence. Your birthday was "terrible" because your best friend did not show up, and the day was ruined! You may even think your friend does not like you now, or that your friendship is over.

In this example, one negative event ruined the entire day. Sadly, someone trapped in all or nothing thinking will find problems in all situations. Nothing is good enough, and they will choose to be miserable. All or nothing thinking translates into all realms of life, including work, school, and relationships.

Reframing All or Nothing Thinking

Reframing is the process of challenging a negative thought, making it positive and more acceptable. Reframing is difficult as it needs to be done right as the thought forms. Waiting too long does not work, as one negative thought often leads to another, leaving the person overwhelmed.

To reframe a thought, first, note the type of thought and the feeling behind it. For our example above, the thought is: "My birthday was ruined because my friend did not show up!". A feeling attached may be of disappointment, anger, both, or something else. Knowing the thought, and how you feel, begins the process of changing how you view the thought.

Once you know the feeling, you can step back and begin to think about it rationally. How was your time with your other friends? Did you enjoy the activities? Did you get any nice gifts? These thoughts begin to challenge your initial thought, becoming more positive.

Next, take the original negative thought, and make it more positive. One example would be:

"I felt disappointed my friend did not show up, but the rest of my day was good, and overall it was not a bad day."

Notice the feeling included, as you can still feel angry or disappointed, but without the extremes.

Last, make a conscious choice to move on and focus on something else. Do not sit and obsess over the disappointment. Move on and do something else to distract yourself from the thought. Often ANTS repeat, meaning you will have to reframe more than once. If you work this process, over time you will notice you are not as upset and are more able to adapt to situations.

For today's activity, write down a recent example of All or Nothing thinking. Note the thought and the feelings associated with it. Next, write out the thought in a more positive way. Finish by writing down what you did to distract yourself and move on from the thought.

Overgeneralization

Overgeneralization is using words such as "always" and "never" to describe yourself and your future. These thoughts are associated with future actions, such as getting a job, finding a relationship, or being happy. Overgeneralization is highly destructive, as it limits your ability to see hope in the future.

In truth, overgeneralizations are excuses not to work and grow. By saying we will "never" be successful, we give ourselves permission to quit. Overgeneralization steals our will to try and allows us to remain miserable.

For example, say an employee wants a promotion but fears he will never achieve it. He thinks, "I will never get a promotion, my boss just does not like me enough!". By using never, it is an absolute, a 100% chance of failure. Why try to gain a promotion if it is impossible? Instead, the employee decides to maintain the status quo and never works enough to gain a promotion. By agreeing with this thought, he has doomed himself to failure.

The same can apply to "always." "I will always be stuck in this dead end job without a promotion because my boss does not like me!". As with "never", change is denied, resulting in a self-fulfilling prophecy.

Reframing Overgeneralization Thoughts

Like in our example with All or Nothing Thoughts, reframing works in the same way. First, list the exact thought and the feelings that accompany it. Our feelings for the example above may be despair, frustration, or anger.

Next, take a step back and think about the thought. How do you know your boss hates you? Have you tried to gain a promotion in the past? If there is no room for advancement, have you thought of a different department or company? By asking these questions, you begin to challenge the validity of the thought.

Now, restate the thought in a more positive light.

"I sometimes feel frustrated that I have not gotten a promotion. I will work hard, and if I do not get one this year, I will evaluate my options".

Notice the feeling word in there, and the actions that follow. This thought is much more positive, as it is realistic and notes change.

Now, distract yourself with something important and move on. In our example, this employee can get back to work, with more energy and focus than before. By reframing this thought, the employee does not have permission to give up and be lazy, which may have been a reason for the thought in the first place. Look at an example in your life, and reframe it as you did with All or Nothing Thinking.

Filtering

Filtering is the conscious act of denying the positives of a situation while instead only focusing on the negative. If this sounds like All or Nothing Thinking, you are correct, with the only difference is the conscious choice of denying positives. By stripping away the positive, only negative, depressing content remains.

For example, say an employee completed a report for his boss. His boss reviewed the report and said it was great, except for one part towards the end. His boss recommended he fix the part, then turn in the report. Once alone, the employee became angry over his mistake, and thought the following: "I am such a failure! He hated my report! How could I be so stupid! The entire report is trash!". He then takes the report, tears it up, and then starts to redo it, angry and upset the entire time.

While most of the report was good, this employee could only see the negatives. Feeling angry at himself for his one flaw, he trashes his report and begins anew. He has lost precious time, and likely will do worse on the report. As this is most likely a pattern, his job could be in jeopardy.

Reframing Filtering

Reframing filtering involves focusing on the positives, as well as the negatives. Removing the negatives is counterproductive, as you cannot fix a problem you ignore. Instead, focusing on both positives and negatives is a healthy mix. The reframed thought may be as follows:

"*I feel somewhat agitated about the errors I made in the report, however, my boss liked most of it. I will fix the problems and turn it in, then move on.*".

Notice the feeling, agitated, as well as the action: fixing the mistakes and moving on. See the pattern yet? Reframing works the same way for most negative thoughts. Go ahead and write down your recent example of filtering, and reframe it.

Mind Reading

Can you read minds? No? Then why do you assume you know someone's thoughts? The truth is, we all mind read, more often than we would care to admit. Mind reading is damaging, especially in relationships, when we make assumptions on how someone thinks. Mind reading can change how we act towards them, with devastating consequences.

Take our example for Overgeneralization. Our employee in question believed his boss did not like him, which was his rationale for not being promoted. Often thoughts include multiple types of ANTS. Due to our employee's mind reading, he felt justified in his belief that he would never get a promotion. In reality, he does not know what his boss thinks of him. Making this assumption encourages him to sit and do nothing. The combination of overgeneralization and mind reading lead to a nasty thought that will keep him trapped.

If you think hard enough, you can find numerous instances of mind reading in your life. It is an extremely common thought we all have. Sometimes, we are correct in our assumptions of others. There is nothing wrong is predicting someone's behavior. But we are not talking about behaviors; we are talking about thoughts. Just because you can sometimes predict someone's behavior, does not mean you know how they think.

Reframing Mind Reading

When mind reading, do not automatically assume your thought is correct, or incorrect. Treat it as a question you want answered. Sometimes thoughts can help us learn more about others, even though they may begin negatively. For our example, we will turn the thought into a question we can later answer with observation.

"Does my boss not like me, which may be why I have not gotten promoted? I don't know if he does, but I will watch how he acts towards me and others, and in time I can get an idea. Regardless, I can work to do better, or if not promoted find other employment".

By reframing it into a question, we now have a choice. We can look for an answer or discard the thought and move on. The employee in question can look for confirmation to his question, but no matter the outcome, he will continue to do his best and evaluate his options. Sitting around feeling sorry for himself is not an option, which is common with mind reading.

Think of an instance lately where you were mind reading, and add it to your list, reframing as I have done above.

Should Statements

When was the last time you thought, "I should have ..." or, "he/she should have ... ". Should statements are problematic, as they are meaningless statements that add nothing of value to your life. Often I hear people tell me they "should" have done something. Or someone "should" have been nice to them. Both would be valid statements if we lived in a fair universe. Unfortunately, we do not. Life is not fair, period.

It would be great if we lived in a world where everyone was kind, considerate, and understanding to all around them. Instead, we live in a world with human beings, who have flaws, faults, and problems. As a result, we say bad things, because we have negative, bad thoughts. No amount of political correctness will change that. Should statements are bad, as they take us out of reality, and give us excuses to fail.

For example, say you have the SAT in 3 months. You are not ready, as you have not studied, and did not do very well in class. You often tell yourself, "I should study today for the SAT!" On the surface, this sounds like a positive statement. Should, however, is the incorrect word. You NEED to study for the test, or you will most likely fail. By saying should, you are giving yourself an out, in case you do not feel like studying. Should is a choice, not an absolute. In this example, you will most likely find an excuse not to study, which will continue until the test. When the test arrives, you will realize how ill-prepared you are, and will become mad at yourself. Should statements are permission statements to fail.

Reframing Should Statements

How then, do we say things correctly, if 'should' is a common part of our language? By reframing to a stronger, more command driven word. For example:

"I **will** study for the SAT today. I **will** study chapter's 2-4 in the vocabulary section and take a practice test".

"I will" commands respect. It is a promise to yourself and others. Unless something bad happens that you cannot prevent, you will study for the test. You have no trap door, no permission statement to avoid studying. You will get it done!

At times you may have had problems doing the assignments in this book. You may have thought you "should" create a daily routine, or "should" delete that application from your phone. Over time, if you begin to watch your thoughts, you will be surprised how often you use the word "should." Think of an instance you used "should" lately and add it to your list.

Quick To-Do List

1. Go through each of the 5 ANTS covered in this chapter, making examples and reframing each as you go.

Tomorrow's Focus

Today's chapter was long, as you began to learn about ANTS. We continue tomorrow with the other 5 ANTS on our list. Make sure to complete your assignment, and add this list to your binder. Tomorrow's chapter is also long, so prepare accordingly.

DAY 25: AUTOMATIC NEGATIVE THOUGHTS – PART 2

Today we continue down our list of Automatic Negative Thoughts, also known as ANTS. Like yesterday, we will discuss each one, with examples, concluding with a section on reframing. Your daily activity is to read through this list, then for each ANT, write down an example and reframe it, like you did yesterday.

Magnification

At times, we exaggerate our problems, especially to ourselves. We get so caught up in the moment we do not see the big picture. A small problem becomes huge, costing us time and emotional energy. As we spend all our energy on small problems, we neglect the larger, more important ones. Magnification ANTS are common and painful.

There are thousands of possible examples to choose from to demonstrate magnification. A typical example would be a traffic jam. Say you were on your way to work when a wreck shuts down a portion of the freeway. Traffic slows to a crawl, with you stuck in the middle. It could take an hour, maybe more, before you can get to work. You left early for work and gave yourself time in case of this event, but it was not enough. You begin to stress, thinking your boss will be upset, and that you may even get fired.

Sound familiar? Most of us have been in a similar situation. The problem is, magnification often leads to unrealistic expectations. No boss in their right mind is going to fire an employee for being late once due to an accident. Sometimes, bad things happen in life outside of our control. If your boss is unrealistic, you may need to consider different employment!

If you have chosen to accept the magnification ANT, you have become stressed and upset. You arrive at work in a bad mood, which might affect your job performance. You may snap at others, or find it difficult to focus on your work. Your day has been affected by an event outside your control, and you let it. Magnification has won.

Reframing Magnification

When a problem occurs, stop and take a deep breath, and give yourself time to think. Reframing the thought is not difficult if you give yourself time to do so. A possible reframed thought for the example above would look like this:

"While I am feeling annoyed about the traffic jam, It will pass. I will put on music to relax and pass the time. I will call my boss and tell them about the accident. Things will work out."

Like our examples yesterday, begin reframing with the feeling you are experiencing. The goal is to admit your feelings, not bury them. Working with feelings lets them out, with makes keeping control of your emotions easier. By listening to music and calling the boss, the problem has become smaller, not bigger. Beyond this, there is nothing else to do but wait. Write down an example of magnification you have experienced lately. Reframe your example like above.

Guilt

Guilt is a very nasty ANT, and one of the worst on our list. Guilt is tricky, as it can have a positive purpose. When we do something wrong, guilt is our internal consequence. People without guilt are often manipulative, and some may be psychopathic. We all need healthy levels of guilt in our lives to help keep us in check.

The problem is when guilt becomes toxic. Over time, once we have learned from our mistake, we need to let go and move on. Sometimes, depending on the severity of our mistakes, we feel the need to continue to punish ourselves. Excessive guilt leads to a type of self-sabotage that in the end hurts us and others.

We all have had excessive guilt in the past. It is part of being human. The question is, why do we hold onto it, even if it hurts us? Earlier in the book, I made this statement: "**Everything we do helps us in the short-term, even if it harms us in the long term.**". In other words, this excessive guilt gives us some benefit, even as it hurts us.

How could excessive guilt benefit us? Excessive guilt gives us permission to fail, by giving reasons not to try. Change is difficult, especially if one has a long, painful past. It is easy to say there is no hope and believe the problem is too great. Guilt gives us the excuse by telling us that we are bad people, or that it is too difficult. This negative self-talk allows us to sit in our rut and do nothing.

For example, say you have spent the past six years playing an online game, spending 12-14 hours a day. You have decided to quit, and over time you are successful. Excessive guilt, however, tells you that you ruined most of your life, that you will eventually relapse, and that you will never fully move past the addiction. You will always be a failure, and deep down you have not recovered. Sound familiar? Guilt ANTS are ones I have to fight in my daily life, and even once you have gained control of your addiction, you will as well.

Reframing Guilt

It is time to stop living in the past, which is guilt's goal. The past is done, finished. You cannot change it. It is time to accept it and move on. When I get a guilt ANT, I reframe it as follows:

"While I mostly wasted six years of my life playing that game, I can use what I have learned to help others, which means I did not waste it after all. I have learned from it and now can manage my life".

Notice how I admitted to the thought being true. While I was addicted, I was wasting my life. But I have moved on. Now I have used the experience at motivation to help others. Therefore, there is nothing to feel guilty over, I have learned from it.

Even though time has made the process easier, it is by no means easy. Guilt is an ANT you will have to reframe often, even for things long past. Now is the time to let the past go, and focus on your future. As you have completed activities in this book, you know more about your strengths, your needs, and you have begun to work on finding your purpose. These are all positives you cannot let guilt steal. Guilt is a thief that will steal your happiness if you let it.

I want you to write down guilty thoughts you have had about you and your addiction. I want you to reframe them, as I have done above. I want you to reframe them every time they enter your mind.

Labeling

Labeling, or name calling, are negative thoughts often found with guilt and overgeneralization. Labeling is the action of insulting yourself in a way that is demeaning and damaging. Labels often include the following:

- I am so stupid; I will never get it right!
- I am a failure and am worthless!
- I am just a hopeless addict who can never change.
- Who would love a loser like me?
- I am a waste of skin; I should have never been born!
- I am an addict with no hope of change.
- Being an addict, I cannot change; it is not possible!

- I am just a depressed moron.

...

We could fill up 100 pages of these if we wanted to. How many of them sound familiar? By placing a negative label on yourself, you begin to act the part. If you have labeled yourself an addict, with no hope of change, how likely is it you will change? If you feel powerless due to labeling yourself an addict, then why waste your time and just give in to the addiction? These thoughts are likely common.

Yes, you are addicted to electronics, or social media, or games, or whatever your addiction is. However, this label does not **define** who you are! You may have an addiction, but you are more than just an addict. Labels steal your power and rob you of making healthy choices.

Reframing Labeling

The next time you call yourself a name, or label yourself in your mind, stop and take a breath, and begin to reframe it. Below are examples of reframing negative labels:

- I am so stupid; I will never get it right! / "I am not stupid, I just need time and practice to get it right. I need to be more patient with myself".
- I am a failure and am worthless! / "I am not a failure and am not worthless. I know my strengths and weaknesses, and work to improve myself".
- I am just a hopeless addict who can never change. / "I may have an addiction, but I refuse to be hopeless. It will be hard, but I will change!".
- Who would love a loser like me? / "I can learn to love myself, and in time, others will as well. I am no loser because I choose not to be!

On paper, reframing sounds simple, just change the thought and go! In reality, reframing is difficult as it takes focus and energy. It can be very tiring to reframe thoughts all day. Using some of the examples above, list some of the labels you have placed on yourself lately, then reframe them into something positive. While it takes time and work, it is worth the effort.

Emotional Reasoning

In the last chapter, I asked if thoughts are always true. Is the same true for emotions? Sometimes, making decisions on emotions or "gut instinct" works. Often, however, making decisions only based on emotions causes more harm than good. Emotional reasoning is making decisions based on how you feel at the moment, without considering facts.

Emotional Reasoning often leads to stereotyping and racism. How we feel about something becomes more important than facts, or opinions of others. How often do you hear people say "I feel I am right!", or "I know I am right!"? Often, when people make statements like these, they are operating out of emotion.

For example, a waiter working at an Italian restaurant has a bunch of teenagers come in one evening. They order and pay, but leave no tip. The waiter becomes angry and thinks the following: "All teenagers are jerks, they don't tip!". The next time he sees a table with teenagers, he does not provide good service as he assumes they will not tip regardless. They do not tip, reinforcing his belief. Eventually, he begins to hate teenagers and anyone looking young, as he assumes they will not tip and be rude.

Was the waiter correct in his assumption? In his first instance, the teenagers were rude for not tipping, and he is justified to be annoyed. However, he made an emotional decision to stereotype all teenagers. Logically you cannot make assumptions on an entire population of people based on one member. But, logic was not in play, emotion was. Racism, for example, often includes emotional reasoning, which exaggerates a limited truth.

Reframing Emotional Reasoning

Reframing emotional reasoning is difficult as we are often emotional and not thinking clearly. It takes focus and control to push past the anger and aggravation. In our example above, the waiter could have reframed as such:

"I am annoyed at this group of teenagers! Hopefully, the next ones that come in tip. In any case, I will do my job".

Like most reframing examples, include the feeling. Annoyance is realistic in this situation. Even though the waiter is annoyed, he will do his job. He leaves the thought hopeful for a better result in the future.

Pick a situation you have used emotional reasoning and write it down, then reframe it as you did the other ANTS.

Predicting the Future

For our last ANT on our list, we will choose one of the worst. While predicting the future, we make negative assumptions, leading to a lack of effort. Statements such as, "It's hopeless, I will never ..." and "Why try? It is hopeless" are negative and dangerous. By making negative assumptions about our future, we lose our will to try.

Often addicts predict they will always be addicts, choosing not to quit due to difficulty. This act of predicting the future steals their will. Why put in all the time and pain it takes to kick an addiction if it is impossible? As with some of the ANTS we have learned, predicting the future is a permission statement to give up and quit.

The truth is, the future is NOT set, and you have CONTROL in making it. You can choose to let your addiction win, or you can make the sacrifice to change. Predicting the future ANTs steal your ability to shape your future. If you believe the future is hopeless, then why try? Like guilt, predicting the future steals your motivation and hope.

The reverse can also be true when predicting the future in an unrealistically positive way. Statements such as "everything will always turn out right!" and "I will do fine, there will be no problems!" can lead to a lack of effort or preparation. Predicting the future in an unrealistic way leads to denial of problems, which solves nothing. Focusing only on the positive is just as bad as only focusing on the negative.

Reframing Predicting the Future

First, stop and take a step back, and do not believe your lies. You do not know what the future holds, for if you did, you would play the lottery and be rich. None of us know what tomorrow will be. Would you want to? For me, knowing the future would rob me of free will, and I want to shape my future.

For example, if you think you will always be an addict, here is how to reframe it:

"I refuse to believe I will always be an addict. I may be addicted, but I am more than an addiction. I will fight and choose my future!".

Notice the direct attack toward "always"? Be specific and choose your thoughts carefully. Attack words such as never, always, and should. They attack you, so attack back! Do not give in to the lies of negative thoughts. Put some attitude in these thoughts, and let them be motivation. Make sure to focus on your future in these thoughts. You can add in a goal, or something you want in the future that will motivate you.

Today's Activity

Congratulations, you just did it. By writing down your list of 10 negative thoughts, complete with reframing, you have begun the process of challenging your thoughts. Learning to reframe your thoughts is a major step in fighting your addiction. Print out this list and add it to your binder. Let it be a reference point.

Quick To-Do List

1. Complete your list of ANTS, including reframing, then add this to your binder. Study this list often and memorize all the different ANTS.

Tomorrow's Focus

Learning to reframe your ANTS is vital for tomorrow's task. Tomorrow, you are going to remove the most addictive application from your mobile devices. As the application removed is likely your main addiction, you will need all you have learned so far to succeed. Study your list of ANTS, and do not forget to journal. Reframing ANTS in your journal is a good way to work through them.

DAY 26: LIMITING ACCESS PART 4

It is time for you to remove your most addictive digital activity from your daily life. You have removed applications from your mobile devices and have created a healthy daily routine. It is time to finish this process by removing your main addiction. Removing your most addictive application will be difficult. It is common to have fears such as, "what will I do with my time?" and "how can I live without it?". Hopefully, while working this book, you are ready to make this choice. You still have access to this application during your two-hour window, but during your day to day activities, you will be free from it. The act of removing this application may be challenging.

Use Your Coping Skills

Today you will need all the coping skills you have learned so far. Conducting grounding exercises often will help you with the moments of anxiety and panic attacks. While panic attacks are extreme, some people experience them when extremely stressed. Removing this application will likely be a very stressful experience, one you will need your coping skills to manage. Meditating before and after you remove the application will help clear your mind.

Today's Activity

It is time to remove the application from your mobile devices. Remember to combat any ANTS that may come up during this process. Reframe them like you learned the past two days and do not let them stop you from completing your task. I suggest you remove the apps or activity in the following order:

1. Meditate for 15 minutes.
2. Gather all mobile devices.
3. Conduct a grounding exercise.
4. Remove the application from all mobile devices.
5. Conduct another grounding exercise.
6. Meditate again for 15 minutes.
7. Engage in one of your new hobbies you recently learned or call a friend or family member.

Once you have removed the application, how do you feel? Do you feel anxiety? Anger? Do you have a sense of relief? Of Panic? No matter how you feel, do not try to bury these feelings. You need to be aware of how you feel now that you have removed the application. The reason most people become addicts is they do not know how to handle pain. Uncomfortable feelings and emotions are pain, which often leads to unhealthy coping skills. The pain you are feeling now needs to be experienced and dealt with, or there is a good chance you will relapse or switch to a different addiction.

Remember, you still have access to this application within your two-hour window at night. During this time you can use the application. However, if you find you relapse often, or you cannot stop thinking of this application, you may need to remove it from your life completely. Some addictions are too powerful to allow access. You may have to make the choice to cut them from your life and never go back.

For the rest of the day, do something you enjoy from your new list of hobbies while you are not in your 2-hour window of electronics usage. During this period of usage you can engage in this application, but be sure to limit your time for two hours. Over time this will become a habit, and during the day you will have more important tasks to focus on.

Quick To-Do List

1. Using the order listed above, remove the final application from your mobile devices.

Tomorrow's Focus

Congratulations, you are nearly done with this book. You have learned more about who you are, about the consequences of your addiction, and how to limit your access to electronics. Tomorrow, you will engage in your final social activity. You have done a lot in the past month and are on your way to being able to control your life. Take a small break, as with all the work you have done in the past few days; you have earned it.

DAY 27: SOCIAL INTERLUDE PART 2

Today is an easy day after all the work you have put in the past three days. Today's activity is simple: you are going to make plans to see a friend, family member, or meetup.com group. As you have finished locking down your mobile devices, it is time to continue becoming more social, so you have more activities and plans with others.

You most likely will not be able to schedule something for today. If you cannot, schedule something for the future, but contact a friend or family member and talk to them about themselves and their lives.

Focus on Others

For most addicts, it is difficult to focus on others when the needs for the addiction are so great. Often addicts are called "selfish" and rightfully so. Part of the recovery process is to learn to listen and interact with others. When I was addicted to my game, I neglected my real world friends much of the time. I neglected my online friends as well, as I often would ignore them for my in-game tasks. Part of my recovery was learning to listen and communicate my feelings with others. Without this, I would not have recovered to the point where I would have been able to resist the game.

When you are with friends, family, or others, take a step back and think about them. Think about their lives, goals, dreams, and what they want out of life. Ask how you can be a greater part of their lives, and how you can help. Sometimes a friend only has to give time and attention to be helpful. The more you listen and are helpful with others, the more time and energy they will spend in helping you.

Today's Activity

Go ahead and make plans with family or friends. It would be a good idea to look back at meetup.com and see if there are any new group meetings, or if there are other groups for you to join. A realistic goal would be two to three social events per week. The more you are out in the real world, the easier it will be to interact and open up. If you continue to have social anxiety, use your coping skills, such as grounding or equal breathing, and reframe any ANTS that get in the way.

For the rest of your day, focus on your new hobbies, and continue journaling. Remember your coping skills and your daily routine.

Quick To-Do List

1. Make arrangements to see a friend, family member, or meetup.com group. If you cannot schedule anything today, talk to a friend or family member, focusing on them.

Tomorrow's Focus

Much change has occurred in your life. You have taken the first step into independence from your addiction. Tomorrow, we will enter the final phase: maintenance. For our final three days, we will focus on all you have learned so far, as well as how you can maintain your recovery. You have done well. Do something nice for yourself, and keep it up!

PART 3: MAINTENANCE

DAY 28: YOUR FINAL DAILY ROUTINE

As this book comes to a close, you have learned about yourself, your addiction, and how to create a final daily routine. This routine will be one you follow every day, regardless of the day of the week. It is designed to give you the flexibility to live life, as well as having the structure to help resist addiction.

If you have been completing your daily assignments in this book, then you are already living your final routine. If not, look through this list, and work through the book to catch up. Below is a summary of what your day will look like, from start to finish.

Mornings

When you wake up each morning, you are going to perform one of the coping skills you have learned. The choice is yours, pick one that works best for you and begin your day with it.

Next, make a list of all your goals for the day. These goals can include work related tasks, household chores, social tasks and hobbies. You can make this list right when you get up, or once you have completed hygiene-related tasks.

If you eat breakfast, make sure your phone or any electronic device is not at the table. While eating, do not use electronics devices. When you go to work, school, or anyplace, make sure to keep your phone in the trunk of the car unless you need to use the GPS. You can keep the phone in your glove compartment, as long as you will not be tempted to use it while driving.

Afternoons

While at work, school, or any social event, work to maintain control over your phone. You have removed your most five addicted applications, so distractions should be limited.

Be diligent and make sure you do not replace one application for another. It will be tempting to play new games, or join more social media applications. Be mindful of your usage and make sure you are not creating a new addiction.

If you find your phone distracting, put it in a drawer or someplace with a lock. The time it takes to unlock the drawer may give you enough time to distract yourself from the urge. If this does not work, store your phone in your vehicle and then every few hours check it for any missed calls.

Grounding techniques are good if you find yourself distracted. Do a quick grounding exercise then get back on task. Taking walks is another way to help gain focus. Do not give yourself time to access your phone for social media or games. You are in public and need to focus on the goals you set in the morning. Save this time for your two hours in the evening.

Keep track of your progress in the afternoon, checking off your goals as you complete them. Writing down your goals is important, so you can physically check them off and see progress. The extra motivation may do wonders for your day.

Once your work, school, or social event is complete, head home, remembering to keep your phone in the trunk or glove compartment. You may feel an urge to check all your messages before you leave. You may do so, but only text messages and phone calls. Social media applications can wait until you are at home in your two-hour window.

Evenings

When you arrive at home, work on getting dinner ready. If you live with family or friends, spend time with them and ask them about their day and how they are doing. You may feel tempted to get on your computer and binge. Fight this urge, instead focusing on social relationships. If you live alone, calling a family member or friend for 5-10 minutes works as well.

Once dinner is complete, complete a grounding or equal breathing exercise. Using your coping skills will help keep you focused, so you do not binge the rest of the night. Once complete, you may begin your two-hour window. Have a clock or a timer nearby, so you can see how much time is passing. You can play games, visit social media, or watch a video. Your time is yours, and you have earned it.

Once your two-hour window is complete, complete another grounding or equal breathing exercise. Next, work on your non-electronic hobbies you have found. Spend the rest of the night in these hobbies until an hour before you go to bed.

Next, get out your journal and write down what you have experienced today. Make sure to discuss the thoughts you have had, noting and reframing ANTS that stick out. Your journal can be a couple of paragraphs daily. It does not need to be a book.

Next, complete a meditation exercise to help clear your mind. You can do this before or after your hygiene-related tasks. Once meditation and hygiene are complete, go to bed, making sure no electronics are in your room. Make sure you go to bed and wake up the same time daily, to form a habit.

On evenings where you have social events, feel free to conduct them. If it eats into your electronics time, this is ok. More time with friends and less time with electronics are preferred. Remember, your electronics time does not transfer, meaning you cannot make up missed hours later.

Today's Activity

Continue to follow this routine, making sure to follow it as closely as possible. If life gets in the way, that is fine. No routine is 100% permanent. For the next 90 days work to follow this routine, making sure to add in social events, such as meetup.com groups and time with friends and family.

Quick To-Do List

1. Follow the daily routine you have created, making sure you complete it daily. Make adjustments when necessary.

Tomorrow's Focus

When your daily routine completed, you are ready to take stock in all you have learned about yourself. This month has included extreme change, and to end it, you need to know what you have learned. Tomorrow, you will write down your overall experiences so that you can refer to them later.

DAY 29: WHAT HAVE YOU LEARNED?

As you have completed this journey, what have you learned about yourself? Was the experience what you expected, or was is completely different? What did you learn about your addiction, and how can you use this knowledge to fight it?

One of the main points of this book is to help you know who you are, and what you want for your future. No addiction is the same, regardless of substance or behavior. Your struggle with addiction is unique.

Below is a list of questions I want you to answer about yourself and your experience while working this book:

- Do I truly believe I am addicted to electronics, or do I still have doubts? If I have doubts, is it because I fear change?
- How has my addiction affected my life? What consequences have I faced?
- What have I gained from my addiction?
- What needs does my addiction supply, and what other activities can I do to fulfill those needs?
- What strengths do I possess that I did not consider before?
- What weakness do I have, and for each, how will I improve them?
- What is the purpose for my life, and how will I achieve it?

- What healthy coping skills do I practice that help me the most?
- Was I able to monitor my time online, and am I still doing so?
- Was I able to complete the tasks of this book? If so, did I do them the day of, or did I have to catch up?
- On most days, did I complete my daily routine? What parts were the hardest?
- What activity or task was the most difficult to complete?
- How often do I have urges to be on electronics? What times of day are the worst?
- Was I able to join groups on meetup.com? How were the group experiences?

- What is the most important thing I learned about myself?

Today's Activity

While this list may seem like a lot, it is critical to answering all the questions above. You need to evaluate yourself in this process so that you can value from it. Be honest with your answers, you are the only person who will see them.

If some of the questions are difficult to answer, or if some of the answers were not up to expectations, relax. I do not expect perfection, and neither should you. Some days you may have struggled or refused to complete the tasks. This struggle helps define the problem and teaches you more about yourself. Complete the list above, be honest, and take enjoyment on the parts you completed well.

Quick To-Do List

1. Answer all questions above, even if the answers are unpleasant. Put this list in your binder.

Tomorrow's Focus

While tomorrow ends your journey in this book, your struggle with addiction will continue. Tomorrow you will focus on your goals for the future, both short and long term. Goals are important for motivation and focus and are vital for success when battling addiction. Continue your daily routine and finish up those questions!

DAY 30: GOALS FOR YOUR FUTURE

You did it; you reached the end of this book. By answering the questions yesterday, you know the struggles you faced while working this book. Today, we focus on the future, as your future is what you will make of it. If you want to be successful, in time you will find success. There will be struggles and sometimes you will fail, but this is part of life. For today's activity, you will write down your goals for the future and put them in your binder, and over time you will modify them as life changes.

Next 30 Days

For the next month, what goals do you have for yourself? How will your life be different than it is now? Will you still be working to control your addiction? What changes will you make to continue on your recovery?

While working this book, your life is likely much different than it was 30 days ago. What do you want to accomplish in the next month? Some suggestions are to engage in 2-3 social events per week, with friends, family or meetup.com groups. Going through this book again is highly recommended, as you will reinforce what you have learned. Learning a new hobby or taking on a new task at work is also recommended.

Whatever goals you make, make them for yourself. Making goals to please others is pointless, as you will not have the motivation to complete them. Visualize how you want your life to be in the next 30 days, and write it down.

Three Months

What do you want your life to look like three months from now? What tasks do you want to accomplish? How often will you use electronics three months from now? Will you be able to maintain the skills you have learned in this book?

Be specific in these goals. You may need to spend some time thinking about them. Who do you want to be three months from now? Have you thought more about your purpose, and if so, are you working toward it? Much can change in three months. The more successes you have, the better you will feel about yourself. Once you experience feelings of success, you will want more.

Six Months

Half a year from now, how do you envision your life? Maybe a change in jobs is in order. Maybe finding a job is on your list. Going back to school may be a consideration. Whatever your goals are, make sure they align with the purpose you are working to discover. Whatever your goals, list them, and list the actions needed to make them happen. For example, if finding a relationship is your goal, how will you achieve it? Will you attend more meetup.com groups to meet people? Will you combat social anxiety so that you can talk to people in public? Will you work on beginning conversations and introducing yourself? For any goal, write out a plan on how you will achieve it.

One Year

Sometimes it is difficult to imagine what life will be life in a year or more. Many people refuse to make plans, as they believe whatever goals they set will be pointless, as life will get in the way. Life does get in the way, but goals need to be flexible. A year from now, who do you want to be? Will you be someone who has mastered their addiction and is living life? Will you be able to be on social media, or be able to play a game, and not binge? Will you be able to have social relationships and not feel the need to be online every waking hour? If you are not in a relationship, will you be on one a year from now? Whatever your goals, write them down, with actions you will take to achieve them.

5 Years and Longer

In five years, how will you imagine your life? Will you have a relationship? Will you have a family? Where do you want to live? Have you found your purpose, and are you living it? Will you have moved on from your addiction and are now free to use electronics in a healthy way? While it is impossible to have answers to these questions, asking them is important, as you need a long term plan for your life.

Determine major life goals you would like to complete within five years and write them down. Keep them in your binder and refer to them every few months. Ask yourself if you are making progress toward them, and if not, what needs to change so you do. You have all the tools available to be successful. Your future is completely up to you. It is time to choose, your life, or your addiction to the Internet. Choose wisely.

Today's Activity

Make realistic goals for each of the time periods above. Expect them to change the farther out into the future you go. Each time you complete a goal, give yourself the freedom to celebrate, as you have earned it.

Quick To-Do List

1. Make goals for all the time periods above, focusing on yourself, your addiction, and your purpose.

Tomorrow's Focus

I suggest starting over with this book and focus on the tasks you did not complete or the ones you found difficult. If it takes you ten tries to complete this book, it will be worth it. If you relapse and binge on electronics, do not despair. It is common for addicts to slip. The good thing is you can pick yourself back up and continue. Do not let any guilt ANTS win if this happens. Read the book again and make sure to live by your new daily routine. Keep practicing your coping skills and keep planning for your future. If you are seeing a therapist, continue, or if not, find a therapist that can help you continue with your recovery.

I want to thank you for reading this book. If you have comments, thoughts, or suggestions, please feel free to visit my website at https://nathandriskell.com. I plan to revise this book at least every two years. If there is something you would like added, let me know! If you have any specific questions, you can e-mail me, and I will work to answer them promptly. If you are in the Houston / Cypress area, I specialize in treating Internet Addiction in all forms, including gaming, social media, gambling, and pornography. I will work with you to create a specific plan for your recovery. Good luck, and be confident in yourself and your future!

Logbook: Hours Spent Online

To download the logbook, click this link below:

Logbook Link: http://nathandriskell.com/internet-addiction-kicking-habit/logbook.xlsx

Note: The logbook is an Excel file, with tabs for each day you work this book. You can copy tabs and make new days if you wish to expand on it.

Automatic Negative Thoughts (ANTS)

If you wish to learn more about Automatic Negative Thoughts (ANTS), please visit the website of Dr. Daniel G. Amen, M.D. He came up with the concept of ANTS and has resources that can help you learn to manage your thoughts better. To visit is website, click the link below:

3 Quick Steps To Stop Negative Thinking Now: http://danielamenmd.com/3-quick-steps-to-stop-negative-thinking-now/

Needs List

The needs list provided on Days 10-11 was created by the Center for Nonviolent Communication:

CONTACT INFORMATION

If you have any questions, comments or suggestions, please feel free to contact me. I have a private practice in the Houston / Cypress area, and I specialize in treating Internet Addiction & High Functioning Autism. If you live in the Houston area and would like to make an appointment, contact me below. If you are outside of Houston and would like to find a therapist who can help you with Internet or Gaming Addiction, please contact me, as I can help direct you to other professionals.

Nathan Driskell: Asperger's & Internet Addiction Specialist
Phone: 832-559-3520
Address: 17510 Huffmeister Rd. Suite #103 Cypress, TX 77429
Website: https://nathandriskell.com

Made in the USA
San Bernardino, CA
24 February 2019